Sir Gawain
and the
Green Knight,
Patience, and Pearl

SIR GAWAIN
AND THE
GREEN KNIGHT,
PATIENCE,
AND PEARL

Verse Translations

MARIE BORROFF
Yale University

W · W · Norton & Company · New York · London

Grateful acknowledgment is made for permission to quote from Emily Dickinson, #1109—reprinted by permission of the publishers and the Trustees of Amherst College from *The Poems of Emily Dickinson*, Thomas H. Johnson, ed., Cambridge, Mass.: The Belknap Press of Harvard University Press, Copyright © 1951, 1955, 1979 by the President and Fellows of Harvard College; and from Robert Frost "Stopping by Woods on a Snowy Evening," from *The Poetry of Robert Frost*, edited by Edward Connery Lathem, Copyright 1923, © 1969 by Henry Holt and Co., copyright 1951 by Robert Frost. Reprinted by permission of Henry Holt and Company, LLC.

The text of this book is composed in Caledonia
with the display set in Albertus.
Composition by PennSet, Inc.
Manufacturing by Courier Companies, Inc.

Library of Congress Cataloging-in-Publication Data

Gawain and the Grene Knight.
    Sir Gawain and the Green Knight ; Patience ; and Pearl : verse translations / by Marie Borroff.
        p. cm.
    Includes bibliographical references (p.).

    ISBN 0-393-97658-0

    1. English poetry—Middle English, 1100–1500—Modernized versions. 2. Gawain (Legendary character)—Romances. I. Title: Sir Gawain and the Green Knight ; Patience ; Pearl. II. Borroff, Marie. III. Patience (Middle English poem) IV. Pearl (Middle English poem) V. Title: Patience. VI. Title: Pearl. VII. Title.

PR1972.G35 A35 2000
821'.1—dc21   00-061616

W. W. Norton & Company, Inc., 500 Fifth Avenue, New York, N.Y. 10110
www.wwnorton.com

W. W. Norton & Company Ltd., Castle House, 75/76 Wells Street,
London W1T 3QT

2 3 4 5 6 7 8 9

Contents

Note

Throughout this book, the Bible is quoted in the Douay-Rheims version, based on the Latin Vulgate version in which it was known to the poet. References to the Authorized, or King James, version, are marked "A.V."

Acknowledgments

My first and abiding debt is to Helge Kökeritz, John C. Pope, and E. Talbot Donaldson, professors of English at Yale in the 1950s, from whom I acquired the knowledge of Old and Middle English and English philology that made this book possible. John Pope and Talbot Donaldson were the tutelary spirits of my translations, first of *Sir Gawain* and then of *Pearl*. While translating *Pearl*, I received helpful suggestions and criticisms from John Freccero, Robert B. Burlin, and A. Bartlett Giamatti and was fortunate in having the assistance in research of M. Teresa Tavormina, who brought to my attention the late medieval bridal crown used in the jacket design of the book. I owe a special debt to Sherry Reames for the thoroughgoing criticism, laced with encouragement, that gave a needed impetus to my work on *Pearl* in the eleventh hour.

My translation of *Patience* is dedicated to Professor Dorothee Metlitzki, in acknowledgment of our friendship and in gratitude to her for sharing with me her knowledge of the original poem and its biblical source.

Marie Borroff
New Haven, Connecticut
November 1999

General Introduction

Sometime between 1350 and 1400 C.E., during the lifetime of Chaucer but far to the northwest of Chaucer's London, a scribe copied four poems into a single manuscript. Conforming to the usual practice of his time, he left them untitled and without attribution to an author. This manuscript alone testifies to their existence. We know them by the names modern editors have given them, *Pearl, Purity* (also called *Cleanness*), *Patience*, and *Sir Gawain and the Green Knight*; they appear in the manuscript in that order. Among scholars having expertise in the Middle English period, there is general agreement that they are the work of a single person, known as the *Gawain*- or *Pearl*-poet. They represent, collectively, an outstanding literary achievement, establishing their author as a figure transcending in importance the late medieval period in which he wrote.

Though it seems certain that a single author wrote all the poems, they differ greatly from one another in subject and form. *Pearl* is a monologue, spoken by a man who mourns, inconsolably, the loss of a precious "pearl without a spot." A maiden appears to him in a dream, and he recognizes her as the pearl he thought he had lost. Speaking to him from the spiritual plane to which she has been translated after her death on earth, she leads him to see that what was truly of value in her exists forever and that he, as a faithful Christian, can hope to be reunited with her in heaven. *Purity* and *Patience* are homilies in verse, that is, they resemble sermons designed to give instruction. The subject of *Purity* is not so much the virtue named in the title as the corresponding sin of uncleanness or filth, which is said to infuriate God above all else and whose chief exemplar for the poet is sexual relations between males. In the course of expounding his theme, the poet retells several Old Testament stories showing how an angry God has punished the unclean, including the inhabitants of Sodom and Gomorrah. In *Patience*, the poet, paraphrasing the Old Testament Book of Jonah, illustrates the contrast between human impatience, exemplified by Jonah, and the patience of God. *Sir Gawain*, the one secular poem of the four, is a romance in which one of the most famous knights of King Arthur's court undergoes a protracted, mystifying, and discomfiting ordeal. He survives it, but not without committing a dishonorable deed that humiliates and infuriates him in retrospect, although his friends at court find it merely laughable.

The poems represent two traditions in English verse: rhyming and alliterative. *Pearl* belongs to the first of these; it is written in sections of five twelve-line stanzas having an elaborate rhyme scheme. Repetition of key words in the last lines of all the stanzas within a section and verbal linkages between one section and the next further complicate its design. *Purity* and *Patience* represent the alliterative tradition in English, which goes back to the Old English period and died out during the fifteenth century. They are written in the "long alliterative line" marked by groups of stressed words beginning with the same letter, and they make use of an inherited vocabulary and phraseology that are part of the tradition. *Sir Gawain* combines rhymed and alliterative verse. It is composed in blocks or "paragraphs" of alliterating lines, each followed by a followed by a two-syllable "bob" joined by rhyme to a four-line stanza of short rhyming lines called the "wheel."

Description and narration in all four poems are governed by an imagination that contemplates with intimate sympathy the experiences of human beings (and, at times, of other living creatures), seeing them always as defined and constrained by circumstance, including the spatial and temporal "frames" within which they take place.

Sir Gawain and the Green Knight

Introduction

Sir Gawain and the Green Knight is not only the finest of the four poems usually attributed to the *Gawain*-poet; it is a literary work of the highest importance in its own right. In it, the poet has interwoven a number of strands to form a complex and fascinating design: the literary tradition of alliterative poetry in English, with its store of inherited poetic words and formulaic phrases; the body of stories, widely known in late medieval times, that recounted the adventures of King Arthur and his knights, including those involving Sir Gawain himself; the duties and obligations of the faithful Christian as governed by the institutional church; the conceptions of knightly honor and of *fin'amour* or *amour courtois*, called "courtly love" in English, that had developed in medieval culture; and, finally, the status of the knightly profession in the real late-fourteenth-century world of the poet.

The plot of the poem, with its elements of the supernatural and of amorous intrigue, reflects the treatment that the originally Celtic Arthurian legends had received at the hands of such medieval French poets as Chrétien de Troyes (late twelfth century). But the poem is a product of the late fourteenth century in England, at a time when the relationship of devoted loyalty between a knight and a single lord was becoming somewhat old-fashioned, slowly giving way to rootless military professionalism. Even Chaucer's knight, who personifies faithfulness and honor and has served worthily in "his lord's war," has also fought in Turkey for "the Lord of Palatye," a Muslim. The old ideal of knightly honor figures conspicuously in the plot of the poem. When Sir Gawain becomes a guest at Hautdesert, he becomes one of the knights of that household, explicitly accepting his host as his liege lord (1039–41). Should he respond to the amorous advances of the lord's wife, he would be not only a sinner in the eyes of the church but a traitor in terms of the feudal ethic. The poet insists on the fact that the virtues symbolized by Gawain's emblem, the pentangle, pertain to him by virtue of his knighthood; he is "to his word most true / And in speech most courteous knight" (638–39). After Gawain's second encounter with the Green Knight, when he realizes that he has fallen somewhat short of perfection, he accuses himself of having behaved in a way "contrary . . . / To largesse and loyalty belonging to knights" (2380–81). The Green Knight affirms his merit in the same terms: Sir Gawain, as against "other gay knights," is like a pearl compared to white peas (2364–65). In part, then, the meaning of the poem consists in its affirmation of an old ideal threatened by change.

The Story

The main story elements of which the plot of *Gawain* is composed derive ultimately from folklore, but the poet himself probably encountered them in French or Latin literary versions, and he was surely the first to combine them. The opening action of the poem retells the story of the "Beheading Game" (traditionally so called), in which an unknown challenger proposes that one of a group of warriors volunteer to cut off his head, the stroke to be repaid in kind at some future date; the hero accepts this challenge and at the crucial moment of reprisal is spared and praised for his courage. Later action incorporates the "Temptation Story," in which an attractive woman attempts to seduce a man under circumstances in which he is bound to resist her, and the "Exchange of Winnings," in which two men agree to exchange what each has acquired during a set period of time. In the plot of *Gawain* these three stories are intricately linked: the hero, having contracted to accept a presumably mortal return stroke from the Green Knight's ax, sets out to meet him, as instructed, at the Green Chapel on New Year's Day. He is unable to find out where the Green Chapel is; instead, he comes upon a magnificent castle where he is sumptuously entertained and later induced by his host to enter on an agreement to exchange winnings at the end of each of three successive days. The host's beautiful wife visits his bedchamber on each of the three mornings and makes amorous overtures toward him; he finally accepts from her, and conceals, a green girdle said to have the power of making its wearer invulnerable. All these plots are resolved at once in the last part of the poem, as Sir Gawain and the Green Knight meet once more. When the poem ends, the most honored knight in the world, famed alike as a courageous warrior and a courteous lover, is proved fallible. His faulty act includes cowardice, because it was brought about by fear of death; covetousness, because it involved the desire to possess a valuable object; and treachery, because it resulted in a breach of faith with the host whose liege-man Gawain had sworn himself to be. To these shortcomings the poet adds a breach of courtesy as this most gracious of knights, confronted with his own fallibility, gives way to anger.

The *Gawain* poet, a master of juxtapositions, has constructed from these separable story elements a whole far greater than the sum of its parts. The castle in which Sir Gawain is entertained is vividly real; its architecture is in the latest Continental style, its court is elegant and gay; its comfortable accommodations and sumptuous fare are as welcome as those of a modern luxury hotel. Yet it is also the mysterious castle that has appeared out of nowhere, shining and shimmering like a mirage, in direct response to Gawain's prayer to the Virgin on Christmas Eve, and it is a way-station on the road to certain death. This shadow hangs over the Christmas festivities, into whose blithe spirit the knight enters as fully as courtesy obliges him to do, and over the high comedy of the bedchamber scenes, in which he not only must refuse the lady's advances but must manage to do so without insulting her. There is a profound psychological truth in the fact that he passes all these tests successfully and at the same time fails the most important one of all: the most dangerous temptation is that which presents itself unexpectedly, as a side issue, while we are busy resisting another. Gawain accepts the belt because he recognizes in it a marvelously appropriate device for evading imminent danger, "a jewel for his jeopardy." At the same time, his act may well seem a way of granting the importunate lady a final favor while evading her amorous invitation. Its full meaning as a cowardly, and hence covetous, grasping at life is revealed to him only later, and with stunning force.

To all this the poet has added three magnificently depicted hunting scenes in which the host, on the three successive days of Gawain's temptation, pursues the deer, the boar, and the fox. It is obvious that these episodes are thematic parallels with the bedchamber scenes, where Gawain is on the defensive and the lady figures as an entrapping huntress, and the relation between the final hunt of the fox and Gawain's ill-fated ruse in concealing the belt is equally apparent. These values are, as it were, inherent in the very presence of the three hunts in the poem, but the poet has also, by his handling of them, added to the dramatic effect of the successive episodes of the narrative. Each hunt is divided in two, enclosing the bedchamber scene of that day like the two halves of a pod. As each one opens, it presents a picture of vigorous, unhampered, and joyous activity, with the host as the central figure dominating the action. From each of these openings we move suddenly to the bed surrounded by curtains, where noise is hushed and space is confined. Nothing could more enhance our sympathetic identification with the hero, whose scope of action is as hedged about morally and socially as it is physically. Each encounter between knight and lady is followed by the conclusion of the corresponding hunt, scenes of carnage and ceremonial butchery that come with all the logic of a violent dream after dutiful constraints.

The "meaning" of the hunting scenes must finally be judged in terms of our experience of them, an experience in which perhaps the most salient quality is that of sheer delight: the joy inherent in physical sport at its best, when a demanding physical activity is carried on with skill, in fine weather, among loyal companions. This joy, though innocent, is of the body, bringing into play that aspect of human beings in which they are one with all animals. The narrator's keen sense of this joy is a part of his love of the physical world, a love manifest also in his knowledge of and delight in "all trades, their gear and tackle and trim," and in that sympathy with animals which leads him to adopt sympathetically the point of view of the hunted creatures and to imagine the suffering inflicted by wind and sleet upon the wild things of the forest. Insofar as we are made to share this attitude we are placed on the side of mortality itself and can thus, with the Green Knight, forgive Gawain for his single act of cowardice: what he did was done not out of sensual lust but for love of life—"the less, then, to blame." In the context of this affectionate sympathy, Gawain's own violent anger at the revelation of his fault must itself be viewed with amusement, as part of his human fallibility. Yet the underlying moral is serious; the pride implicit in accepting one's own reputation has been humbled; the lesson Gawain has been taught applies *a fortiori* to the court of which he is the most honored representative and, by further extension, to all men.

The Traditional Style

In "The Metrical Forms" (p. 166), I describe the normal or basic form, defined in terms of patterns of stress and alliteration, of the long alliterating line as we find it in the works of the *Gawain*-poet. I then give examples of some variations on the basic form, and I present specimen scansions, in Middle and modern English, of two passages that produce contrasting but equally felicitous metrical effects. Poets no longer write alliterative poetry in this technical sense, although the modern language lends itself as well to the requirements of the form as the *Gawain*-poet's Middle English. More directly relevant to the full meaning of the poem is its verbal style—that is, the vocabulary, phraseology, and descriptive techniques generally—that were taken over by the poet from his precursors in the alliterative tradition. In this respect, *Sir Gawain and the Green Knight* resembles in descriptive and verbal style the other alliterative poems composed at the same time, though such was the poet's artistry that, while recounting the events of his narrative in thoroughly traditional fashion, he was able to stamp them with his own imaginative imprint.

Old English (Anglo-Saxon) poetry was written in alliterative verse. It is my view that late Middle English alliterative verse, as represented in the works of the *Gawain*-poet, is the lineal descendant of its precursor. It must have evolved, largely unrecorded, over a period of several centuries, during which it underwent modifications of form reflecting changes in the spoken language. Old English alliterative verse, in turn, must ultimately have descended from a body of "prehistoric" alliterative verse composed in the language common to the Germanic peoples when they were a single cultural entity in northwest Europe, long before the Angles, Saxons, and Jutes invaded England in the fifth century C.E. This early poetry preserved in memory the exploits, historical or legendary or both, of ancestral folk heroes: chieftains and warriors famous for their loyalty, strength, and courage. The vocabulary and phraseology of this poetry was shaped by the interplay between its traditional subject matter and the technical requirements of the verse: the necessity of providing, in each line, an alliterative link between at least two words, one in each half of the line, or, more commonly, among three such words, two in the first half-line and one in the second. The result was a repertoire, transmitted from poet to poet, of groups of synonymous words expressing important meanings: nouns such as *hero, warhorse, sword,* and *battle,* and verbs such as *to ride, to speak,* and *to look.* Of particular importance, alongside these, was a set of adjectives signifying the admirable qualities inherent "by definition" in those who figured in the stories: courage, strength, loyalty, and virtue in general. When the scope of alliterative poetry widened during the Middle English period to include romantic as well as martial themes, new groups of words were added that expressed meanings relevant to ladies, lovers, and wooing and that signified attributes such as beauty, courtesy, gaiety, and graciousness. As the language continued to change, a number of these words, though they were preserved in the existing poems and used anew by successive generations of poets, died out in the spoken language of everyday life. They thus became "poetic words," taking on a literary aura of the sort that words like *beauteous* (vs. *beautiful*) and *dwell* (vs. *live*) have for us today.

The poet's knowledge of these vocabularies was an important part of his craft. Because the words in any group of synonyms began with a number of different letters, he could usually draw from a given group a word that alliterated with another word he needed to use in the same line. He could also, when referring to his hero, select from his store of qualitative adjectives one that began with a useful alliterating letter, because the praiseworthy attributes these adjectives signified were, theoretically at least, applicable at any point in the narrative. These same strategies are available to a modern translator. When Sir Gawain rides into the grounds of the great castle that has appeared before him on Christmas Eve, as if in answer to his prayer of contrition, the poet tells us that by chance he chose the main path and was led by it to the end of the drawbridge that crossed the moat: "That broght bremly [quickly] the burne [warrior] to the bryge ende." *Burne* is one of the traditional synonyms for "man"; like most of the poetic words used by the poet for alliterating purposes, it became obsolete in early modern English. Here it provides a link with the needed word *bridge.* A modern equivalent for the line can be devised with the aid of a qualitative adjective beginning with *b*: "That brought the bold knight to the bridge's end."

We can best understand the contribution made by these features of the traditional style to the meaning of the poem if we look at them, so to speak, from the opposite direction: from the reader's side rather than the author's. They may have entered the poet's language as a technical aid, but once present in it, they suffuse it with the expressive values they have acquired by virtue of their association with the traditional stories and their removal, as poetic words, from everyday life. They help characterize the narrator of the story as dignified in manner and as a knowledgeable advocate for the characters who stand for "our" values—the values implied by such adjectives as *good, loyal,* and *brave.* We can think of him as the spokesman for their reputation, and this role is particularly important in a poem whose plot hinges on reputation, first that of the knights of King Arthur's court and later that of Sir Gawain himself. His manner throughout the poem retains its time-honored dignity. The story he has to tell, however, belies it. It includes the humiliation of the knightly company and its king by an outlandish, obstreperous, and jeeringly dismissive stranger, and the exquisite physical and social unease of the hero as he lies naked under the covers while chatting with the beautiful and seemingly amorous lady who sits, uninvited, inside the curtains of his bed. As a result, stock words and phrases in the language of the original sometimes produce, in context, effects that are difficult to describe though easy to feel, taking on a hollow ring or attracting insidiously inappropriate meanings. The adjective *stiff,* for example, had in Middle English a poetic meaning, "resolute," as well as its most common modern one. When King Arthur, as he stands around waiting to hear or see something wonderful before joining in the feast, is called "the stiff king himself," the narrator surely means the adjective as an honorific, but the less dignified modern meaning intrudes itself and, once invoked, cannot be dispelled. (I have tried to approximate this effect by using the similarly ambiguous word *stout,* as if the king were not only stalwart but a little portly.) At other times, the meaning of one of the traditional adjectives of praise is disturbingly unsuitable for the narrative context in which it appears, as when the narrator says, in my translation, that "many a champion bold" among King Arthur's knights was afraid to answer the Green Knight's first question (the language of the original works similarly). Disparities of this same sort arise later, when the narrator uses in reference to Sir Gawain, at moments when he is sorely tried, one of a group of adjectives signifying the cheerfulness of mien a courteous knight is expected to display at all times. When the wife of his host, on the morning of her first visit, claims to have taken him captive and threatens to "bind him in his bed," he manages a courteous reply, but at that moment the appellation "Gawain the blithe" (1213), applied to him by the narrator, seems jarringly unsuitable. Later in their conversation, when he must yet again devise a polite reply to yet another of her thinly veiled sexual overtures, he is referred to as "the merry man."

History originated as poetry. It served two purposes: to commemorate (poetic form being a mnemonic aid) and to praise. The author of *Sir Gawain* begins his poem with a historical summary going back to the destruction of Troy. He speaks of the founding of the kingdom of Britain and of the kings who ruled there, among whom he singles out Arthur. And he bestows praise as he goes along: the ancestral British warriors were bold and fierce, doers of "many a deed most dire" (22), Arthur was the "most courteous" of all

British kings (26), and the "marvel" we are going to hear about is matchless among the wonders of his reign (28–29). At the end of this passage, the poet refers unmistakably to the poetic tradition in which he himself participates: he has heard this tale "in hall," where it was "linked in measures meetly / By letters tried and true" (35–36), that is, composed in alliterative verse. (The original has "Locked in loyal letters.") It is not surprising, then, that the background of his story, including the adventures that have given rise to the reputation of King Arthur's knights, is not what we would call history, but rather a body of fictional narratives to which his own will make a further contribution.

As his story opens, we see the values of the past perpetuated in the present. The court in its every aspect is all that tradition dictates that it should be, a happy place on a hill, peopled by the noblest of knights, the loveliest of ladies, and the comeliest of kings. At the New Year's feast that opens the poem, Arthur has remained standing; he will not sit down until a tale "of some fair feat or fray" is told him, or a stranger knight asks his permission to "join in jousting" with a knight of his household. This custom of the king's is well-known in earlier Arthurian literature, and his expectations, as the poet delineates them, lie safely within traditional bounds. What happens, however, is something else again. The Green Knight is, in every conceivable respect, strange: unlike any other knight in clothing, in gear, in abundance of beard and hair, and, needless to say, in color. Strangest of all, the overpowering vividness of his presence, as communicated to us by the poet, gives him a kind of brute reality that seems to be lacking in the idealized knights he has come to challenge. When he explains his visit in terms of the "praise" he has heard of this assembly, and speaks of Camelot as the "house . . . / Whose fame is so fair in far realms and wide" (309–10), he seems to be referring not to actual deeds worthy of commendation but to stories that may or may not be true.

Fame and Fiction

The interplay between reality and story initiated in the opening episode of the poem becomes prominent again in the adventures of its hero. Sir Gawain, as we learn when he becomes a guest at the castle of Lord Bertilak, is preeminent in fame even among King Arthur's knights. The lord is elated and the men of his household are overjoyed when they find that it is Gawain who is to be their guest, for they know of him as a "paragon," one who is "praised without end" (913). Among his praiseworthy qualities, one is especially conspicuous. We find it attributed to him in Chaucer's *Canterbury Tales*, when the Squire, narrating his own tale, describes the salutation of the knight on the steed of brass to those present at the court of Cambyuskan:

even "Gawayn, with his olde curteisye, Though he were comen ayeyn out of
Fairye" could not have improved on it (V[F] 95–97). The lord's wife alludes
to this aspect of his fame when she addresses him during her first visit to
his bed:

> For as certain as I sit here, Sir Gawain you are,
> Whom all the world worships, whereso you ride;
> Your honor, your courtesy are highest acclaimed
> By lord and by ladies, by all living men.   (1226–29)

More disconcertingly, she uses it to chide him: he cannot be Sir Gawain,
she tells him, because Sir Gawain would have "claimed a kiss, by his cour-
tesy" before they parted (1300). On her visit the following morning, she uses
the same tactic: it is strange, if he is indeed Sir Gawain, that he "cannot act
in company as courtesy bids" (1483). This disparity between his reputation
and his actions, it turns out, consists in his having failed not only to kiss her
but to use, in conversation with her, "the language of love," wooing her and
then instructing her, during her husband's absence, in "new pastimes" such
as may or may not be suitable for a married woman to engage in with a
house guest. Here again, reality and fiction tend to merge. In a number of
the Arthurian romances, Gawain is portrayed as amorous and fickle, ever
susceptible to the charms of women though permanently committing himself
to none. The lady, evidently aware of this aspect of the tradition, questions
the identity of the man beside her as if he were a movie star—a sex symbol
who might or might not live up to his image on the screen.

Courtesy, as the lord's wife seems to conceive of it, is the art of flattering
a lady to lure her into amorous interplay; its goal is seduction. But the Ga-
wain we see in action in the poem is not the womanizer his bedside visitor
takes him to be. He is the Gawain who bears the pentangle on his shield,
and the set of five virtues signified by that emblem includes *cortaysye* side
by side with *clannes* or purity (653; I translate "pure mind and manners").
Moreover, each of the "five fives" symbolized by the pentangle, including
the five wounds on the cross and the five joys of the Virgin, is linked insep-
arably with all the rest in an "endless knot," so that a breach in one would
be a breach in the whole design (630, 655–61). For this Gawain, there is no
conflict between courtesy and chastity—except, ironically, in the third bed-
room scene. Here, the lady is more desirable, and her invitation to love-
making more explicit, than ever. There is no question of his becoming her
lover, however his mortal flesh may be stirred by her beauty (1760–62), for
to allow himself to do so would be sinful (1774). In refusing her, he must
take the lesser risk of appearing discourteous (1773). The poet avails himself
of more than one opportunity to insist that the courtesy of the Gawain he
has in mind is free from any taint of lewdness even when he speaks of love.
Having learned the identity of their guest, the men of the lord's household
look forward to observing his behavior:

With command of manners pure
He shall each heart imbue;
Who shares his converse, sure,
Shall learn love's language true.

(924–27; cf. 1010–15)

Affinities with *Pearl*

At this point, anyone who knows the other works ascribed to the *Gawain*-poet will be irresistibly reminded of *Pearl*. By virtue of its derivation, the word *courtesy* signifies the way people behave at a court, and the author of *Pearl* imagines the bliss of eternity as a feast in a court reigned over by a lord, excelling earthly courts in degree rather than in kind. As the *Pearl*-maiden, in successive speeches, corrects the misapprehensions of the dreamer, courtesy becomes a central concept. The word appears for the first time in section VIII, which begins with the maiden's invocation to the Virgin as "courteous queen"; it is the link word of that section, appearing at the end of every stanza. In the sense in which the maiden uses it, it signifies the bond whereby every soul in heaven rejoices in the bliss of every other. Though Sir Gawain is earthbound, and ultimately proves fallible, courtesy as he embodies it has affinities with the spiritual courtesy imagined by the author of *Pearl*.

The design of the pentangle, too, has a counterpart in *Pearl*: the continuity that warrants its being called the "endless knot," the fact that every part of it interweaves with every other without a break, corresponds to the "endless" circularity of the single great pearl that symbolizes the freedom of the heavenly realm from linear time. The image of the circle in *Pearl* has its counterpart in the image of the line in the Parable of the Vineyard, which has a beginning and an end corresponding to "lowest" and "highest" in more abstract scales of degrees of rank and value. (See the "Introduction" to *Pearl*, p. 116, and the notes to section X, p. 162.) And the two poems have a further similarity. If we look in *Sir Gawain* for an image that is a counterpart to the pentangle as the line is a counterpart to the circle in *Pearl*, we find it in the knotted girdle that binds the lady's outer garment about her in the third bedroom scene. This knot is not endless; in fact, the poet speaks, when he refers to it later, of the gold that gleams on its "ends" (2039). The lady undoes it and, in so doing, causes Sir Gawain to break the "endless knot" of the pentangle by failing to uphold two of his five emblematic virtues: generosity and faithfulness (2379ff.). A third virtue, the courtesy for which he is famous, is angrily jettisoned after all has been revealed: berating himself for falling into the lady's trap, the knight disparages women in general, associating himself with a long line of biblical figures who have yielded to their "wiles" and wishing that there were some way to love them and not believe them. We need look no further than *The Wife of Bath's Prologue* to see that his speech is typical of medieval antifeminist discourse.

Finally, *Sir Gawain* resembles *Pearl* in that each was composed in accordance with a numerical design. Each, too, is "circular," in that its final line echoes its opening (this latter device is found, with a difference, in *Patience* as well). I discuss the numerical aspect of *Pearl* in the "Introduction" to that poem; its key number is twelve, a number of particular importance in the symbolic lore of Christianity. In *Sir Gawain*, the key number is five. It is symbolized by the pentangle, each of whose points stands for a set of five items, the total being five squared, or twenty-five. Kent Hieatt has shown that the number twenty-five also figures in the length of the poem as a whole. The echo of line 1 occurs in line 2525, which is followed by the concluding five lines of the bob and wheel.° Why five? In thinking about this question, I am reminded of the fact that the first of the five fives symbolized by the pentangle is the five senses. When the Green Knight judges and absolves Sir Gawain, he ascribes the knight's lapse of good faith to love of life—"the less, then, to blame." Though no one has described the joys of life after death more memorably than this poet, he ends his "best book of romance" by assuring its hero, and, indirectly, its audience, that life on earth, too, is worth our love.

The Translation

It has seemed to me that a modern verse-translation of *Sir Gawain and the Green Knight* must fulfill certain requirements deriving from the nature of the original style. First, it must so far as possible preserve the formulaic character of the language. This not infrequently involves repetition of wording within the poem itself; for example, the poet uses the same phrase in describing the original entrance and exit of the Green Knight, and the translator ought to do the same; the poem opens and closes with much the same wording; there are verbal reminiscences of the original beheading scene in the episode at the Green Chapel, and so on. But beyond this, the style of the translation must, if possible, have something of the expectedness of the language of the fairy tale, with its "handsome princes" and "beautiful princesses," its opening "once upon a time" and its closing "they lived happily ever after"—though any suggestion of whimsy or quaintness in so adult and sophisticated a literary work would be, to say the least, out of place. In trying to meet this condition I have incorporated into the translation as many as possible of the formulas still current in the language. The reader will recognize such phrases as "tried and true," "winsome ways," "hot on his heels,"

° It is a curious fact that in *Sir Gawain*, as in *Pearl*, the total number of stanzas is 101.

and others; these have, I think, served my turn well, though many such phrases were too restricted in use to the realm of colloquial speech to be suitable in tone.

Second, the diction of the translation must, so far as possible, reflect that of the original poem. The traditional style as it appears in late Middle English embraces a wide range of kinds of words, from strictly poetic terms comparable in status to *wherefore* or *in sooth* today to words used primarily in the ordinary speech of the time, many of which have not descended into the modern language. But the style does not juxtapose discordant elements of diction for humorous effect, like the poetry of Ogden Nash, for example. The level varies, but with subtle shifts of tone from solemnity to realistic vigor. I began the translation with the general notion that because the poet used words that were poetic in his time I could do the same, but I realized after a time that I was using such words where the original was colloquial, and that in any case the connotations of poetic diction for us have crucially altered. I finally used literary words only where it seemed to me that their effect was unobtrusive, and I similarly made use of distinctively colloquial words where the resultant effect seemed to me similar to that of the original. My translation thus includes both the archaic *lo!* and the colloquial *swap* (which appears, in fact, in the original), and I have tried to imitate the poet in modulating from one level to the other, avoiding at one extreme a pseudo-medieval quaintness and, at the other, an all too homely familiarity.

A modern translation of *Sir Gawain* must, so far as possible, reproduce both the metrical variety of the original and its cumulative momentum or "swing." These aspects of the poem are discussed in some detail in "The Metrical Forms" (p. 166ff.).

Like all translators of poetry, I have been faced with the basic difficulty of reproducing the sense of the poem in lines that satisfy the requirements of metrical form and, beyond this, are effective as rhythmic combinations of words. Like all translators of poetry, I have constantly had to compromise, sometimes forced away from literal rendition by the exigencies of the meter, sometimes foregoing an attractive phrase or cadence for the sake of a more faithful rendition, sometimes finding myself able to have it both ways. I have tried to follow the poet as much in what he does not say as in what he does say, refraining from explicitness where he leads the reader, tantalizingly, to surmise. And I have done my best during the entire process of translation to attend carefully and respectfully to the exact sense of the poem at every turn, though I have inevitably had at times to decide what was essential in a given line—what must be literally reproduced at all costs—and to content myself with substitutes of, I hope, equivalent value, for the rest. Where I have been forced to deviate from the original, I have sometimes made the pleasurable discovery that in changing one line I have echoed another elsewhere in the poem.

I believe that I have in the end produced a translation more *like* the original than the others I have seen, though the success of the translation as a modern poem is for its readers to judge. It must inevitably fall short of the great achievement of the *Gawain* poet, but, like the page in the Christmas carol, I have continually found warmth and strength in treading in his footsteps.

Sir Gawain and the Green Knight[†]

Part I

Since the siege and the assault was ceased at Troy,[1]
The walls breached and burnt down to brands and ashes,
The knight that had knotted the nets of deceit
Was impeached for his perfidy, proven most true,
It was high-born Aeneas and his haughty race   5
That since prevailed over provinces, and proudly reigned
Over well-nigh all the wealth of the West Isles.
Great Romulus to Rome repairs in haste;
With boast and with bravery builds he that city
And names it with his own name, that it now bears.   10
Ticius to Tuscany, and towers raises.
Langobard in Lombardy lays out homes,
And far over the French Sea, Felix Brutus
On many broad hills and high Britain he sets,
       most fair.   15
    Where war and wrack and wonder
    By shifts have sojourned there,
    And bliss by turns with blunder
    In that land's lot had share.

And since this Britain was built by this baron great,   20
Bold boys bred there, in broils delighting,
That did in their day many a deed most dire.
More marvels have happened in this merry land
Than in any other I know, since that olden time,
But of those that here built, of British kings,   25
King Arthur was counted most courteous of all,
Wherefore an adventure I aim to unfold,
That a marvel of might some men think it,
And one unmatched among Arthur's wonders.

† Notes for *Sir Gawain and the Green Knight* appear on pages 75–78.

If you will listen to my lay but a little while,   30
As I heard it in hall, I shall hasten to tell
anew.
As it was fashioned featly
In tale of derring-do,
And linked in measures meetly   35
By letters tried and true.

This king lay at Camelot at Christmastide;
Many good knights and gay his guests were there,
Arrayed of the Round Table rightful brothers,
With feasting and fellowship and carefree mirth.   40
There true men contended in tournaments many,
Joined there in jousting these gentle knights,
Then came to the court for carol-dancing,
For the feast was in force full fifteen days,
With all the meat and the mirth that men could devise,   45
Such gaiety and glee, glorious to hear,
Brave din by day, dancing by night.
High were their hearts in halls and chambers,
These lords and these ladies, for life was sweet.
In peerless pleasures passed they their days,   50
The most noble knights known under Christ,
And the loveliest ladies that lived on earth ever,
And be the comeliest king, that that court holds,
For all this fair folk in their first age
were still.   55
Happiest of mortal kind,
King noblest famed of will;
You would now go far to find
So hardy a host on hill.

While the New Year was new, but yesternight come,   60
This fair folk at feast two-fold was served,
When the king and his company were come in together,
The chanting in chapel achieved and ended.
Clerics and all the court acclaimed the glad season,
Cried Noel anew, good news to men;   65
Then gallants gather gaily, hand-gifts to make,
Called them out clearly, claimed them by hand,
Bickered long and busily about those gifts.
Ladies laughed aloud, though losers they were,
And he that won was not angered, as well you will know.   70
All this mirth they made until meat was served;
When they had washed them worthily, they went to their seats,

The best seated above, as best it beseemed,
Guenevere the goodly queen gay in the midst
On a dais well-decked and duly arrayed   75
With costly silk curtains, a canopy over,
Of Toulouse and Turkestan tapestries rich,
All broidered and bordered with the best gems
Ever brought into Britain, with bright pennies
                              to pay.   80
              Fair queen, without a flaw,
              She glanced with eyes of grey.
              A seemlier that once he saw,
              In truth, no man could say.

But Arthur would not eat till all were served;   85
So light was his lordly heart, and a little boyish;
His life he liked lively—the less he cared
To be lying for long, or long to sit,
So busy his young blood, his brain so wild.
And also a point of pride pricked him in heart,   90
For he nobly had willed, he would never eat
On so high a holiday, till he had heard first
Of some fair feat or fray some far-borne tale,
Of some marvel of might, that he might trust,
By champions of chivalry achieved in arms,   95
Or some suppliant came seeking some single knight
To join with him in jousting, in jeopardy each
To lay life for life, and leave it to fortune
To afford him on field fair hap or other.
Such is the king's custom, when his court he holds   100
At each far-famed feast amid his fair host
                              so dear.
              The stout king stands in state
              Till a wonder shall appear;
              He leads, with heart elate,   105
              High mirth in the New Year.

So he stands there in state, the stout young king,
Talking before the high table of trifles fair.
There Gawain the good knight by Guenevere sits,
With Agravain à la dure main on his other side,   110
Both knights of renown, and nephews of the king.
Bishop Baldwin above begins the table,
And Yvain, son of Urien, ate with him there.
These few with the fair queen were fittingly served;
At the side-tables sat many stalwart knights.[2]   115

Then the first course comes, with clamor of trumpets
That were bravely bedecked with bannerets bright,
With noise of new drums and the noble pipes.
Wild were the warbles that wakened that day
In strains that stirred many strong men's hearts.   120
There dainties were dealt out, dishes rare,
Choice fare to choose, on chargers so many
That scarce was there space to set before the people
The service of silver, with sundry meats,
                              on cloth.   125
                    Each fair guest freely there
                    Partakes, and nothing loth;
                    Twelve dishes before each pair;
                    Good beer and bright wine both.

Of the service itself I need say no more,   130
For well you will know no tittle was wanting.
Another noise and a new was well-nigh at hand,
That the lord might have leave his life to nourish;
For scarce were the sweet strains still in the hall,
And the first course come to that company fair,   135
There hurtles in at the hall-door an unknown rider,
One the greatest on ground in growth of his frame:
From broad neck to buttocks so bulky and thick,
And his loins and his legs so long and so great,
Half a giant on earth I hold him to be,   140
But believe him no less than the largest of men,
And that the seemliest in his stature to see, as he rides,
For in back and in breast though his body was grim,
His waist in its width was worthily small,
And formed with every feature in fair accord   145
                              was he.
                    Great wonder grew in hall
                    At his hue most strange to see,
                    For man and gear and all
                    Were green as green could be.   150

And in guise all of green, the gear and the man:
A coat cut close, that clung to his sides,
And a mantle to match, made with a lining
Of furs cut and fitted—the fabric was noble,
Embellished all with ermine, and his hood beside,   155
That was loosed from his locks, and laid on his shoulders.
With trim hose and tight, the same tint of green,

His great calves were girt, and gold spurs under
He bore on silk bands that embellished his heels,
And footgear well-fashioned, for riding most fit.   160
And all his vesture verily was verdant green;
Both the bosses on his belt and other bright gems
That were richly ranged on his raiment noble
About himself and his saddle, set upon silk,
That to tell half the trifles would tax my wits,   165
The butterflies and birds embroidered thereon
In green of the gayest, with many a gold thread.
The pendants of the breast-band, the princely crupper,
And the bars of the bit were brightly enameled;
The stout stirrups were green, that steadied his feet,   170
And the bows of the saddle and the side-panels both,
That gleamed all and glinted with green gems about.
The steed he bestrides of that same green
                                    so bright.
                         A green horse great and thick;   175
                         A headstrong steed of might;
                         In broidered bridle quick,
                         Mount matched man aright.

Gay was this goodly man in guise all of green,
And the hair of his head to his horse suited;   180
Fair flowing tresses enfold his shoulders;
A beard big as a bush on his breast hangs,[3]
That with his heavy hair, that from his head falls,
Was evened all about above both his elbows,
That half his arms thereunder were hid in the fashion   185
Of a king's cap-à-dos,[4] that covers his throat.
The mane of that mighty horse much to it like,
Well curled and becombed, and cunningly knotted
With filaments of fine gold amid the fair green,
Here a strand of the hair, here one of gold;   190
His tail and his foretop twin in their hue,
And bound both with a band of a bright green
That was decked adown the dock with dazzling stones
And tied tight at the top with a triple knot
Where many bells well burnished rang bright and clear.   195
Such a mount in his might, nor man on him riding,
None had seen, I dare swear, with sight in that hall
                                    so grand.
                         As lightning quick and light
                         He looked to all at hand;   200

It seemed that no man might
His deadly dints withstand.

Yet had he no helm, nor hauberk neither,
Nor plate, nor appurtenance appending to arms,
Nor shaft pointed sharp, nor shield for defense,   205
But in his one hand he had a holly bob
That is goodliest in green when groves are bare,
And an ax in his other, a huge and immense,
A wicked piece of work in words to expound:
The head on its haft was an ell long;   210
The spike of green steel, resplendent with gold;
The blade burnished bright, with a broad edge,
As well shaped to shear as a sharp razor;
Stout was the stave in the strong man's gripe,
That was wound all with iron to the weapon's end,   215
With engravings in green of goodliest work.
A lace lightly about, that led to a knot,
Was looped in by lengths along the fair haft,
And tassels thereto attached in a row,
With buttons of bright green, brave to behold.   220
This horseman hurtles in, and the hall enters;
Riding to the high dais, recked he no danger;
Not a greeting he gave as the guests he o'erlooked,
Nor wasted his words, but "Where is," he said,
"The captain of this crowd?⁵ Keenly I wish   225
To see that sire with sight, and to himself say
          my say."
                He swaggered all about
                To scan the host so gay;
                He halted, as if in doubt   230
                Who in that hall held sway.

There were stares on all sides as the stranger spoke,
For much did they marvel what it might mean
That a horseman and a horse should have such a hue,⁶
Grow green as the grass, and greener, it seemed,   235
Than green fused on gold more glorious by far.
All the onlookers eyed him, and edged nearer,
And awaited in wonder what he would do,
For many sights had they seen, but such a one never,
So that phantom and faerie the folk there deemed it,   240
Therefore chary of answer was many a champion bold,
And stunned at his strong words stone-still they sat

In a swooning silence in the stately hall.
As all were slipped into sleep, so slackened their speech
       apace.   245
    Not all, I think, for dread,
    But some of courteous grace
    Let him who was their head
    Be spokesman in that place.

Then Arthur before the high dais that entrance beholds, 250
And hailed him, as behooved, for he had no fear,
And said "Fellow, in faith you have found fair welcome;
The head of this hostelry Arthur am I;
Leap lightly down, and linger, I pray,
And the tale of your intent you shall tell us after." 255
"Nay, so help me," said the other, "He that on high sits,
To tarry here any time, 'twas not mine errand;
But as the praise of you, prince, is puffed up so high,
And your court and your company are counted the best,
Stoutest under steel-gear on steeds to ride, 260
Worthiest of their works the wide world over,
And peerless to prove in passages of arms,
And courtesy here is carried to its height,
And so at this season I have sought you out.
You may be certain by the branch that I bear in hand 265
That I pass here in peace, and would part friends,
For had I come to this court on combat bent,
I have a hauberk at home, and a helm beside,
A shield and a sharp spear, shining bright,
And other weapons to wield, I ween well, to boot, 270
But as I willed no war, I wore no metal.
But if you be so bold as all men believe,
You will graciously grant the game that I ask
      by right."
    Arthur answer gave 275
    And said, "Sir courteous knight,
    If contest here you crave,
    You shall not fail to fight."

"Nay, to fight, in good faith, is far from my thought;
There are about on these benches but beardless children, 280
Were I here in full arms on a haughty steed,
For measured against mine, their might is puny.
And so I call in this court for a Christmas game,
For 'tis Yule and New Year, and many young bloods about;

If any in this house such hardihood claims,   285
Be so bold in his blood, his brain so wild,
As stoutly to strike one stroke for another,
I shall give him as my gift this gisarme noble,
This ax, that is heavy enough, to handle as he likes,
And I shall bide the first blow, as bare as I sit.   290
If there be one so wilful my words to assay,
Let him leap hither lightly, lay hold of this weapon;
I quitclaim it forever, keep it as his own,
And I shall stand him a stroke, steady on this floor,
So you grant me the guerdon to give him another,   295
                    sans blame.
              In a twelvemonth and a day
              He shall have of me the same;
              Now be it seen straightway
              Who dares take up the game."   300

If he astonished them at first, stiller were then
All that household in hall, the high and the low;
The stranger on his green steed stirred in the saddle,
And roisterously his red eyes he rolled all about,
Bent his bristling brows, that were bright green,   305
Wagged his beard as he watched who would arise.
When the court kept its counsel he coughed aloud,
And cleared his throat coolly, the clearer to speak:
"What, is this Arthur's house," said that horseman then,
"Whose fame is so fair in far realms and wide?   310
Where is now your arrogance and your awesome deeds,
Your valor and your victories and your vaunting words?
Now are the revel and renown of the Round Table
Overwhelmed with a word of one man's speech,
For all cower and quake, and no cut felt!"   315
With this he laughs so loud that the lord grieved;
The blood for sheer shame shot to his face,
                    and pride.
              With rage his face flushed red,
              And so did all beside.   320
              Then the king as bold man bred
              Toward the stranger took a stride.

And said "Sir, now we see you will say but folly,
Which whoso has sought, it suits that he find.
No guest here is aghast of your great words.   325
Give to me your gisarme, in God's own name,

And the boon you have begged shall straight be granted."
He leaps to him lightly, lays hold of his weapon;
The green fellow on foot fiercely alights.
Now has Arthur his ax, and the haft grips,   330
And sternly stirs it about, on striking bent.
The stranger before him stood there erect,
Higher than any in the house by a head and more;
With stern look as he stood, he stroked his beard,
And with undaunted countenance drew down his coat,   335
No more moved nor dismayed for his mighty dints
Than any bold man on bench had brought him a drink
      of wine.
    Gawain by Guenevere
    Toward the king doth now incline: 340
    "I beseech, before all here,
    That this melee may be mine."

"Would you grant me the grace," said Gawain to the king,
"To be gone from this bench and stand by you there,
If I without discourtesy might quit this board,   345
And if my liege lady misliked it not,
I would come to your counsel before your court noble.
For I find it not fit, as in faith it is known,
When such a boon is begged before all these knights,
Though you be tempted thereto, to take it on yourself   350
While so bold men about upon benches sit.
That no host under heaven is hardier of will,
Nor better brothers-in-arms where battle is joined;
I am the weakest, well I know, and of wit feeblest;
And the loss of my life would be least of any;   355
That I have you for uncle is my only praise;
My body, but for your blood, is barren of worth;
And for that this folly befits not a king,
And 'tis I that have asked it, it ought to be mine,
And if my claim be not comely let all this court judge,   360
      in sight."
    The court assays the claim.
    And in counsel all unite
    To give Gawain the game
    And release the king outright.   365

Then the king called the knight to come to his side,
And he rose up readily, and reached him with speed,
Bows low to his lord, lays hold of the weapon,

And he releases it lightly, and lifts up his hand,
And gives him God's blessing, and graciously prays   370
That his heart and his hand may be hardy both.
"Keep, cousin," said the king, "what you cut with this day,
And if you rule it aright, then readily, I know,
You shall stand the stroke it will strike after."
Gawain goes to the guest with gisarme in hand,   375
And boldly he bides there, abashed not a whit.
Then hails he Sir Gawain, the horseman in green:
"Recount we our contract, ere you come further.
First I ask and adjure you, how you are called
That you tell me true, so that trust it I may."   380
"In good faith," said the good knight, "Gawain am I
Whose buffet befalls you, whate'er betide after,
And at this time twelvemonth take from you another
With what weapon you will, and with no man else
                    alive."   385
                The other nods assent:
                "Sir Gawain, as I may thrive,
                I am wondrous well content
                That you this dint shall drive."

"Sir Gawain," said the Green Knight, "By Gog, I rejoice   390
That your fist shall fetch this favor I seek,
And you have readily rehearsed, and in right terms,
Each clause of my covenant with the king your lord,
Save that you shall assure me, sir, upon oath,
That you shall seek me yourself, wheresoever you deem   395
My lodgings may lie, and look for such wages
As you have offered me here before all this host."
"What is the way there?" said Gawain, "Where do you dwell?
I heard never of your house, by Him that made me,
Nor I know you not, knight, your name nor your court.   400
But tell me truly thereof, and teach me your name,
And I shall fare forth to find you, so far as I may,
And this I say in good certain, and swear upon oath."
"That is enough in New Year, you need say no more,"
Said the knight in the green to Gawain the noble,   405
"If I tell you true, when I have taken your knock,
And if you handily have hit, you shall hear straightway
Of my house and my home and my own name;
Then follow in my footsteps by faithful accord.
And if I spend no speech, you shall speed the better: 410
You can feast with your friends, nor further trace

                    my tracks.
                Now hold your grim tool steady
                And show us how it hacks."
                "Gladly, sir; all ready,"   415
                Says Gawain; he strokes the ax.

The Green Knight upon ground girds him with care;
Bows a bit with his head, and bares his flesh;
His long lovely locks he laid over his crown,
Let the naked nape for the need be shown.   420
Gawain grips to his ax and gathers it aloft—
The left foot on the floor before him he set—
Brought it down deftly upon the bare neck,
That the shock of the sharp blow shivered the bones
And cut the flesh cleanly and clove it in twain,   425
That the blade of bright steel bit into the ground.
The head was hewn off and fell to the floor;
Many found it at their feet, as forth it rolled;
The blood gushed from the body, bright on the green,
Yet fell not the fellow, nor faltered a whit,   430
But stoutly he starts forth upon stiff shanks,
And as all stood staring he stretched forth his hand,
Laid hold of his head and heaved it aloft,
Then goes to the green steed, grasps the bridle,
Steps into the stirrup, bestrides his mount,   435
And his head by the hair in his hand holds,
And as steady he sits in the stately saddle
As he had met with no mishap, nor missing were
                    his head.
                His bulk about he haled,   440
                That fearsome body that bled;
                There were many in the court that quailed
                Before all his say was said.

For the head in his hand he holds right up;
Toward the first on the dais directs he the face,   445
And it lifted up its lids, and looked with wide eyes,
And said as much with its mouth as now you may hear:
"Sir Gawain, forget not to go as agreed,
And cease not to seek till me, sir, you find,
As you promised in the presence of these proud knights.   450
To the Green Chapel come, I charge you, to take
Such a dint as you have dealt—you have well deserved
That your neck should have a knock on New Year's morn.
The Knight of the Green Chapel I am well-known to many,

Wherefore you cannot fail to find me at last;   455
Therefore come, or be counted a recreant knight."
With a roisterous rush he flings round the reins,
Hurtles out at the hall-door, his head in his hand,
That the flint-fire flew from the flashing hooves.
Which way he went, not one of them knew   460
Nor whence he was come in the wide world

so fair.
The king and Gawain gay
Make game of the Green Knight there,
Yet all who saw it say   465
'Twas a wonder past compare.

Though high-born Arthur at heart had wonder,
He let no sign be seen, but said aloud
To the comely queen, with courteous speech,
"Dear dame, on this day dismay you no whit;   470
Such crafts are becoming at Christmastide,
Laughing at interludes, light songs and mirth,
Amid dancing of damsels with doughty knights.
Nevertheless of my meat now let me partake,
For I have met with a marvel, I may not deny."   475
He glanced at Sir Gawain, and gaily he said,
"Now, sir, hang up your ax, that has hewn enough,"[7]
And over the high dais it was hung on the wall
That men in amazement might on it look,
And tell in true terms the tale of the wonder.   480
Then they turned toward the table, these two together,
The good king and Gawain, and made great feast,
With all dainties double, dishes rare,
With all manner of meat and minstrelsy both,
Such happiness wholly had they that day   485

in hold.
Now take care, Sir Gawain,
That your courage wax not cold
When you must turn again
To your enterprise foretold.   490

Part II

This adventure had Arthur of handsels first
When young was the year, for he yearned to hear tales;
Though they wanted for words when they went to sup,
Now are fierce deeds to follow, their fists stuffed full.

Gawain was glad to begin those games in hall,   495
But if the end be harsher, hold it no wonder,
For though men are merry in mind after much drink,
A year passes apace, and proves ever new:
First things and final conform but seldom.
And so this Yule to the young year yielded place,   500
And each season ensued at its set time;
After Christmas there came the cold cheer of Lent,
When with fish and plainer fare our flesh we reprove;
But then the world's weather with winter contends;
The keen cold lessens, the low clouds lift;   505
Fresh falls the rain in fostering showers
On the face of the fields; flowers appear.
The ground and the groves wear gowns of green;
Birds build their nests, and blithely sing
That solace of all sorrow with summer comes   510
                    ere long.
              And blossoms day by day
              Bloom rich and rife in throng;
              Then every grove so gay
              Of the greenwood rings with song.   515

And then the season of summer with the soft winds,
When Zephyr sighs low over seeds and shoots;
Glad is the green plant growing abroad,
When the dew at dawn drops from the leaves,
To get a gracious glance from the golden sun.   520
But harvest with harsher winds follows hard after,
Warns him to ripen well ere winter comes;
Drives forth the dust in the droughty season,
From the face of the fields to fly high in air.
Wroth winds in the welkin wrestle with the sun,   525
The leaves launch from the linden and light on the ground,
And the grass turns to gray, that once grew green.
Then all ripens and rots that rose up at first,
And so the year moves on in yesterdays many,
And winter once more, by the world's law,   530
                    draws nigh.
              At Michaelmas the moon
              Hangs wintry pale in sky;
              Sir Gawain girds him soon
              For travails yet to try.   535

Till All-Hallows' Day with Arthur he dwells,
And he held a high feast to honor that knight

With great revels and rich, of the Round Table.
Then ladies lovely and lords debonair
With sorrow for Sir Gawain were sore at heart;   540
Yet they covered their care with countenance glad:
Many a mournful man made mirth for his sake.
So after supper soberly he speaks to his uncle
Of the hard hour at hand, and openly says,
"Now, liege lord of my life, my leave I take;   545
The terms of this task too well you know—
To count the cost over concerns me nothing.
But I am bound forth betimes to bear a stroke
From the grim man in green, as God may direct."
Then the first and foremost came forth in throng: 550
Yvain and Eric and others of note,
Sir Dodinal le Sauvage, the Duke of Clarence,
Lionel and Lancelot and Lucan the good,
Sir Bors and Sir Bedivere, big men both,
And many manly knights more, with Mador de la Porte.   555
All this courtly company comes to the king
To counsel their comrade, with care in their hearts;
There was much secret sorrow suffered that day
That one so good as Gawain must go in such wise
To bear a bitter blow, and his bright sword   560
                    lay by.
          He said, "Why should I tarry?"
          And smiled with tranquil eye;
          "In destinies sad or merry,
          True men can but try."   565

He dwelt there all that day, and dressed in the morning;
Asked early for his arms, and all were brought.
First a carpet of rare cost was cast on the floor
Where much goodly gear gleamed golden bright;
He takes his place promptly and picks up the steel,   570
Attired in a tight coat of Turkestan silk
And a kingly cap-à-dos, closed at the throat,
That was lavishly lined with a lustrous fur.
Then they set the steel shoes on his sturdy feet
And clad his calves about with comely greaves,   575
And plate well-polished protected his knees,
Affixed with fastenings of the finest gold.
Fair cuisses enclosed, that were cunningly wrought,
His thick-thewed thighs, with thongs bound fast,

And massy chain-mail of many a steel ring   580
He bore on his body, above the best cloth,
With brace burnished bright upon both his arms,
Good couters and gay, and gloves of plate,
And all the goodly gear to grace him well
     that tide.   585
   His surcoat blazoned bold;
   Sharp spurs to prick with pride;
   And a brave silk band to hold
   The broadsword at his side.

When he had on his arms, his harness was rich,   590
The least latchet or loop laden with gold;
So armored as he was, he heard a mass,
Honored God humbly at the high altar.
Then he comes to the king and his comrades-in-arms,
Takes his leave at last of lords and ladies,   595
And they clasped and kissed him, commending him to Christ.
By then Gringolet was girt with a great saddle
That was gaily agleam with fine gilt fringe,
New-furbished for the need with nail-heads bright;
The bridle and the bars bedecked all with gold;   600
The breast-plate, the saddlebow, the side-panels both,
The caparison and the crupper accorded in hue,
And all ranged on the red the resplendent studs
That glittered and glowed like the glorious sun.
His helm now he holds up and hastily kisses,   605
Well-closed with iron clinches, and cushioned within;
It was high on his head, with a hasp behind,
And a covering of cloth to encase the visor,
All bound and embroidered with the best gems
On broad bands of silk, and bordered with birds,   610
Parrots and popinjays preening their wings,
Lovebirds and love-knots as lavishly wrought
As many women had worked seven winters thereon,
     entire.
   The diadem costlier yet   615
   That crowned that comely sire,
   With diamonds richly set,
   That flashed as if on fire.

Then they showed forth the shield, that shone all red,
With the pentangle portrayed in purest gold.[8]   620
About his broad neck by the baldric he casts it,

That was meet for the man, and matched him well.
And why the pentangle is proper to that peerless prince
I intend now to tell, though detain me it must.
It is a sign by Solomon sagely devised   625
To be a token of truth, by its title of old,
For it is a figure formed of five points,
And each line is linked and locked with the next
For ever and ever, and hence it is called
In all England, as I hear, the endless knot.[9]   630
And well may he wear it on his worthy arms,
For ever faithful five-fold in five-fold fashion
Was Gawain in good works, as gold unalloyed,
Devoid of all villainy, with virtues adorned
               in sight.   635
         On shield and coat in view
         He bore that emblem bright,
         As to his word most true
         And in speech most courteous knight.

And first, he was faultless in his five senses,   640
Nor found ever to fail in his five fingers,
And all his fealty was fixed upon the five wounds
That Christ got on the cross, as the creed tells;
And wherever this man in melee took part,
His one thought was of this, past all things else,   645
That all his force was founded on the five joys
That the high Queen of heaven had in her child.
And therefore, as I find, he fittingly had
On the inner part of his shield her image portrayed,
That when his look on it lighted, he never lost heart.   650
The fifth of the five fives followed by this knight
Were beneficence boundless and brotherly love
And pure mind and manners, that none might impeach,
And compassion most precious[10]—these peerless five
Were forged and made fast in him, foremost of men.   655
Now all these five fives were confirmed in this knight,
And each linked in other, that end there was none,
And fixed to five points, whose force never failed,
Nor assembled all on a side, nor asunder either,
Nor anywhere at an end, but whole and entire   660
However the pattern proceeded or played out its course.
And so on his shining shield shaped was the knot
Royally in red gold against red gules,
That is the peerless pentangle, prized of old

in lore. 665
Now armed is Gawain gay,
And bears his lance before,
And soberly said good day,
He thought forevermore.

He struck his steed with the spurs and sped on his way 670
So fast that the flint-fire flashed from the stones.
When they saw him set forth they were sore aggrieved,
And all sighed softly, and said to each other,
Fearing for their fellow, "Ill fortune it is
That you, man, must be marred, that most are worthy! 675
His equal on this earth can hardly be found;
To have dealt more discreetly had done less harm,
And have dubbed him a duke, with all due honor.
A great leader of lords he was like to become,
And better so to have been than battered to bits, 680
Beheaded by an elf-man, for empty pride!
Who would credit that a king could be counseled so,
And caught in a cavil in a Christmas game?"
Many were the warm tears they wept from their eyes
When goodly Sir Gawain was gone from the court 685
that day.
No longer he abode,
But speedily went his way
Over many a wandering road,
As I heard my author say. 690

Now he rides in his array through the realm of Logres,
Sir Gawain, God knows, though it gave him small joy!
All alone must he lodge through many a long night
Where the food that he fancied was far from his plate;
He had no mate but his mount, over mountain and plain, 695
Nor man to say his mind to but almighty God,
Till he had wandered well-nigh into North Wales.
All the islands of Anglesey he holds on his left,
And follows, as he fares, the fords by the coast,
Comes over at Holy Head, and enters next 700
The Wilderness of Wirral[11]—few were within
That had great good will toward God or man.
And earnestly he asked of each mortal he met
If he had ever heard aught of a knight all green,
Or of a Green Chapel, on ground thereabouts, 705
And all said the same, and solemnly swore
They saw no such knight all solely green

in hue.
Over country wild and strange
The knight sets off anew;   710
Often his course must change
Ere the Chapel comes in view.

Many a cliff must he climb in country wild;
Far off from all his friends, forlorn must he ride;
At each strand or stream where the stalwart passed   715
'Twere a marvel if he met not some monstrous foe,
And that so fierce and forbidding that fight he must.
So many were the wonders he wandered among
That to tell but the tenth part would tax my wits.
Now with serpents he wars, now with savage wolves,   720
Now with wild men of the woods, that watched from the rocks,
Both with bulls and with bears, and with boars besides,
And giants that came gibbering from the jagged steeps.
Had he not borne himself bravely, and been on God's side,
He had met with many mishaps and mortal harms.   725
And if the wars were unwelcome, the winter was worse,
When the cold clear rains rushed from the clouds
And froze before they could fall to the frosty earth.
Near slain by the sleet he sleeps in his irons
More nights than enough, among naked rocks,   730
Where clattering from the crest the cold stream ran
And hung in hard icicles high overhead.
Thus in peril and pain and predicaments dire
He rides across country till Christmas Eve,
                          our knight.   735
              And at that holy tide
              He prays with all his might
              That Mary may be his guide
              Till a dwelling comes in sight.

By a mountain next morning he makes his way   740
Into a forest fastness, fearsome and wild;
High hills on either hand, with hoar woods below,
Oaks old and huge by the hundred together,
The hazel and the hawthorn were all intertwined
With rough raveled moss, that raggedly hung,   745
With many birds unblithe upon bare twigs
That peeped most piteously for pain of the cold.
The good knight on Gringolet glides thereunder
Through many a marsh and mire, a man all alone;
He feared for his default, should he fail to see   750

The service of that Sire that on that same night
Was born of a bright maid, to bring us His peace.
And therefore sighing he said, "I beseech of Thee, Lord,
And Mary, thou mildest mother so dear,
Some harborage where haply I might hear mass   755
And Thy matins tomorrow—meekly I ask it,
And thereto proffer and pray my pater and ave
                    and creed."
                He said his prayer with sighs,
                Lamenting his misdeed;   760
                He crosses himself, and cries
                On Christ in his great need.

No sooner had Sir Gawain signed himself thrice
Than he was ware, in the wood, of a wondrous dwelling,
Within a moat, on a mound, bright amid boughs   765
Of many a tree great of girth that grew by the water—
A castle as comely as a knight could own,
On grounds fair and green, in a goodly park
With a palisade of palings planted about
For two miles and more, round many a fair tree.   770
The stout knight stared at that stronghold great
As it shimmered and shone amid shining leaves,
Then with helmet in hand he offers his thanks
To Jesus and Saint Julian, that are gentle both,
That in courteous accord had inclined to his prayer; 775
"Now fair harbor," said he, "I humbly beseech!"
Then he pricks his proud steed with the plated spurs,
And by chance he has chosen the chief path
That brought the bold knight to the bridge's end
                    in haste.   780
                The bridge hung high in air;
                The gates were bolted fast;
                The walls well-framed to bear
                The fury of the blast.

The man on his mount remained on the bank   785
Of the deep double moat that defended the place.
The wall went in the water wondrous deep,
And a long way aloft it loomed overhead.
It was built of stone blocks to the battlements' height,
With corbels under cornices in comeliest style;   790
Watch-towers trusty protected the gate,
With many a lean loophole, to look from within:
A better-made barbican the knight beheld never.

And behind it there hoved a great hall and fair:
Turrets rising in tiers, with tines at their tops,   795
Spires set beside them, splendidly long,
With finials well-fashioned, as filigree fine.
Chalk-white chimneys over chambers high
Gleamed in gay array upon gables and roofs;
The pinnacles in panoply, pointing in air,   800
So vied there for his view that verily it seemed
A castle cut of paper for a king's feast.
The good knight on Gringolet thought it great luck
If he could but contrive to come there within
To keep the Christmas feast in that castle fair   805
            and bright.
            There answered to his call
            A porter most polite;
            From his station on the wall
            He greets the errant knight.   810

"Good sir," said Gawain, "Wouldst go to inquire
If your lord would allow me to lodge here a space?"
"Peter!" said the porter, "For my part, I think
So noble a knight will not want for a welcome!"
Then he bustles off briskly, and comes back straight,   815
And many servants beside, to receive him the better.
They let down the drawbridge and duly went forth
And kneeled down on their knees on the naked earth
To welcome this warrior as best they were able.
They proffered him passage—the portals stood wide—   820
And he beckoned them to rise, and rode over the bridge.
Men steadied his saddle as he stepped to the ground,
And there stabled his steed many stalwart folk.
Now come the knights and the noble squires
To bring him with bliss into the bright hall.   825
When his high helm was off, there hied forth a throng
Of attendants to take it, and see to its care;
They bore away his brand and his blazoned shield;
Then graciously he greeted those gallants each one,
And many a noble drew near, to do the knight honor.   830
All in his armor into hall he was led,
Where fire on a fair hearth fiercely blazed.
And soon the lord himself descends from his chamber
To meet with good manners the man on his floor.
He said, "To this house you are heartily welcome: 835
What is here is wholly yours, to have in your power

and sway."
"Many thanks," said Sir Gawain;
"May Christ your pains repay!"
The two embrace amain   840
As men well met that day.

Gawain gazed on the host that greeted him there,
And a lusty fellow he looked, the lord of that place:
A man of massive mold, and of middle age;
Broad, bright was his beard, of a beaver's hue,[12]   845
Strong, steady his stance, upon stalwart shanks,
His face fierce as fire, fair-spoken withal,
And well-suited he seemed in Sir Gawain's sight
To be a master of men in a mighty keep.
They pass into a parlor, where promptly the host   850
Has a servant assigned him to see to his needs,
And there came upon his call many courteous folk
That brought him to a bower where bedding was noble,
With heavy silk hangings hemmed all in gold,
Coverlets and counterpanes curiously wrought,   855
A canopy over the couch, clad all with fur,
Curtains running on cords, caught to gold rings,
Woven rugs on the walls of eastern work,
And the floor, under foot, well-furnished with the same.
With light talk and laughter they loosed from him then   860
His war-dress of weight and his worthy clothes.
Robes richly wrought they brought him right soon,
To change there in chamber and choose what he would.
When he had found one he fancied, and flung it about,
Well-fashioned for his frame, with flowing skirts,   865
His face fair and fresh as the flowers of spring,
All the good folk agreed, that gazed on him then,
His limbs arrayed royally in radiant hues,
That so comely a mortal never Christ made
                          as he.   870
              Whatever his place of birth,
              It seemed he well might be
              Without a peer on earth
              In martial rivalry.

A couch before the fire, where fresh coals burned,   875
They spread for Sir Gawain splendidly now
With quilts quaintly stitched, and cushions beside,
And then a costly cloak they cast on his shoulders
Of bright silk, embroidered on borders and hems,

With furs of the finest well-furnished within,   880
And bound about with ermine, both mantle and hood;
And he sat at that fireside in sumptuous estate
And warmed himself well, and soon he waxed merry.
Then attendants set a table upon trestles broad,
And lustrous white linen they laid thereupon,   885
A saltcellar of silver, spoons of the same.
He washed himself well and went to his place,
Men set his fare before him in fashion most fit.
There were soups of all sorts, seasoned with skill,
Double-sized servings, and sundry fish,   890
Some baked, some breaded, some broiled on the coals,
Some simmered, some in stews, steaming with spice,
And with sauces to sup that suited his taste.
He confesses it a feast with free words and fair;
They requite him as kindly with courteous jests,   895
      well-sped.
    "Tonight you fast and pray;
    Tomorrow we'll see you fed."[13]
    The knight grows wondrous gay
    As the wine goes to his head.   900

Then at times and by turns, as at table he sat,
They questioned him quietly, with queries discreet,
And he courteously confessed that he comes from the court,
And owns him of the brotherhood of high-famed Arthur,
The right royal ruler of the Round Table,   905
And the guest by their fireside is Gawain himself,
Who has happened on their house at that holy feast.
When the name of the knight was made known to the lord,
Then loudly he laughed, so elated he was,
And the men in that household made haste with joy   910
To appear in his presence promptly that day,
That of courage ever-constant, and customs pure,
Is pattern and paragon, and praised without end:
Of all knights on earth most honored is he.
Each said solemnly aside to his brother,   915
"Now displays of deportment shall dazzle our eyes
And the polished pearls of impeccable speech;
The high art of eloquence is ours to pursue
Since the father of fine manners is found in our midst.
Great is God's grace, and goodly indeed,   920
That a guest such as Gawain he guides to us here
When men sit and sing of their Savior's birth

                         in view.
              With command of manners pure
              He shall each heart imbue;   925
              Who shares his converse, sure,
              Shall learn love's language true."

When the knight had done dining and duly arose,
The dark was drawing on; the day nigh ended.
Chaplains in chapels and churches about   930
Rang the bells aright, reminding all men
Of the holy evensong of the high feast.
The lord attends alone; his fair lady sits
In a comely closet, secluded from sight.
Gawain in gay attire goes thither soon;   935
The lord catches his coat, and calls him by name,
And has him sit beside him, and says in good faith
No guest on God's earth would he gladlier greet.
For that Gawain thanked him; the two then embraced
And sat together soberly the service through.   940
Then the lady, that longed to look on the knight,
Came forth from her closet with her comely maids.
The fair hues of her flesh, her face and her hair
And her body and her bearing were beyond praise,
And excelled the queen herself, as Sir Gawain thought.   945
He goes forth to greet her with gracious intent;
Another lady led her by the left hand
That was older than she—an ancient, it seemed,
And held in high honor by all men about.
But unlike to look upon, those ladies were,[14]   950
For if the one was fresh, the other was faded:
Bedecked in bright red was the body of one;
Flesh hung in folds on the face of the other;
On one a high headdress, hung all with pearls;
Her bright throat and bosom fair to behold,   955
Fresh as the first snow fallen upon hills;
A wimple the other one wore round her throat;
Her swart chin well swaddled, swathed all in white;
Her forehead enfolded in flounces of silk
That framed a fair fillet, of fashion ornate.   960
And nothing bare beneath save the black brows,
The two eyes and the nose, the naked lips,
And they unsightly to see, and sorrily bleared.
A beldame, by God, she may well be deemed,

of pride!　965
She was short and thick of waist,
Her buttocks round and wide;
More toothsome, to his taste,
Was the beauty by her side.

When Gawain had gazed on that gay lady,　970
With leave of her lord, he politely approached;
To the elder in homage he humbly bows;
The lovelier he salutes with a light embrace.
He claims a comely kiss, and courteously he speaks;
They welcome him warmly, and straightway he asks　975
To be received as their servant, if they so desire.
They take him between them; with talking they bring him
Beside a bright fire; bade then that spices
Be freely fetched forth, to refresh them the better,
And the good wine therewith, to warm their hearts.　980
The lord leaps about in light-hearted mood;
Contrives entertainments and timely sports;
Takes his hood from his head and hangs it on a spear,
And offers him openly the honor thereof
Who should promote the most mirth at that Christmas feast;　985
"And I shall try for it, trust me—contend with the best,
Ere I go without my headgear by grace of my friends!"
Thus with light talk and laughter the lord makes merry
To gladden the guest he had greeted in hall

that day.　990
At the last he called for light
The company to convey;
Gawain says goodnight
And retires to bed straightway.

On the morn when each man is mindful in heart　995
That God's son was sent down to suffer our death,
No household but is blithe for His blessed sake;
So was it there on that day, with many delights.
Both at larger meals and less they were lavishly served
By doughty lads on dais, with delicate fare;　1000
The old ancient lady, highest she sits;
The lord at her left hand leaned, as I hear;
Sir Gawain in the center, beside the gay lady,
Where the food was brought first to that festive board,
And thence throughout the hall, as they held most fit,　1005
To each man was offered in order of rank.
There was meat, there was mirth, there was much joy,

That to tell all the tale would tax my wits,
Though I pained me, perchance, to paint it with care;
But yet I know that our knight and the noble lady   1010
Were accorded so closely in company there,
With the seemly solace of their secret words,
With speeches well-sped, spotless and pure,
That each prince's pastime their pleasures far
                outshone.   1015
          Sweet pipes beguile their cares,
          And the trumpet of martial tone;
          Each tends his affairs
          And those two tend their own.

That day and all the next, their disport was noble,   1020
And the third day, I think, pleased them no less;
The joys of St. John's Day were justly praised,[15]
And were the last of their like for those lords and ladies;
Then guests were to go in the gray morning,
Wherefore they whiled the night away with wine and with mirth,   1025
Moved to the measures of many a blithe carol;
At last, when it was late, took leave of each other,
Each one of those worthies, to wend his way.
Gawain bids goodbye to his goodly host
Who brings him to his chamber, the chimney beside,   1030
And detains him in talk, and tenders his thanks
And holds it an honor to him and his people
That he has harbored in his house at that holy time
And embellished his abode with his inborn grace.
"As long as I may live, my luck is the better   1035
That Gawain was my guest at God's own feast!"
"Noble sir," said the knight, "I cannot but think
All the honor is your own—may heaven requite it!
And your man to command I account myself here
As I am bound and beholden, and shall be, come   1040
                what may."
          The lord with all his might
          Entreats his guest to stay;
          Brief answer makes the knight:
          Next morning he must away.   1045

Then the lord of that land politely inquired
What dire affair had forced him, at that festive time,
So far from the king's court to fare forth alone
Ere the holidays wholly had ended in hall.
"In good faith," said Gawain, "you have guessed the truth: 1050

On a high errand and urgent I hastened away,
For I am summoned by myself to seek for a place—
I would I knew whither, or where it might be!
Far rather would I find it before the New Year
Than own the land of Logres, so help me our Lord!   1055
Wherefore, sir, in friendship this favor I ask,
That you say in sober earnest, if something you know
Of the Green Chapel, on ground far or near,
Or the lone knight that lives there, of like hue of green.
A certain day was set by assent of us both   1060
To meet at that landmark, if I might last,
And from now to the New Year is nothing too long,
And I would greet the Green Knight there, would God but allow,
More gladly, by God's Son, than gain the world's wealth!
And I must set forth to search, as soon as I may;   1065
To be about the business I have but three days
And would as soon sink down dead as desist from my errand."
Then smiling said the lord, "Your search, sir, is done,
For we shall see you to that site by the set time.
Let Gawain grieve no more over the Green Chapel;   1070
You shall be in your own bed, in blissful ease,
All the forenoon, and fare forth the first of the year,
And make the goal by midmorn, to mind your affairs,
                    no fear!
          Tarry till the fourth day   1075
          And ride on the first of the year.
          We shall set you on your way;
          It is not two miles from here."

Then Gawain was glad, and gleefully he laughed:
"Now I thank you for this, past all things else!   1080
Now my goal is here at hand! With a glad heart I shall
Both tarry, and undertake any task you devise."
Then the host seized his arm and seated him there;
Let the ladies be brought, to delight them the better,
And in fellowship fair by the fireside they sit;   1085
So gay waxed the good host, so giddy his words,
All waited in wonder what next he would say.
Then he stares on the stout knight, and sternly he speaks:
"You have bound yourself boldly my bidding to do—
Will you stand by that boast, and obey me this once?"   1090
"I shall do so indeed," said the doughty knight;
"While I lie in your lodging, your laws will I follow."
"As you have had," said the host, "many hardships abroad

And little sleep of late, you are lacking, I judge,
Both in nourishment needful and nightly rest;   1095
You shall lie abed late in your lofty chamber
Tomorrow until mass, and meet then to dine
When you will, with my wife, who will sit by your side
And talk with you at table, the better to cheer
                              our guest.   1100
              A-hunting I will go
              While you lie late and rest."
              The knight, inclining low,
              Assents to each behest.

"And Gawain," said the good host, "agree now to this: 1105
Whatever I win in the woods I will give you at eve,
And all you have earned you must offer to me;
Sweat now, sweet friend, to swap as I say,
Whether hands, in the end, be empty or better."
"By God," said Sir Gawain, "I grant it forthwith!   1110
If you find the game good, I shall gladly take part."
"Let the bright wine be brought, and our bargain is done,"
Said the lord of that land—the two laughed together.
Then they drank and they dallied and doffed all constraint,
These lords and these ladies, as late as they chose,   1115
And then with gaiety and gallantries and graceful adieux
They talked in low tones, and tarried at parting.
With compliments comely they kiss at the last;
There were brisk lads about with blazing torches
To see them safe to bed, for soft repose   1120
                              long due.
              Their covenants, yet awhile,
              They repeat, and pledge anew;
              That lord could well beguile
              Men's hearts, with mirth in view.   1125

Part III

Long before daylight they left their beds;
Guests that wished to go gave word to their grooms,
And they set about briskly to bind on saddles,
Tend to their tackle, tie up trunks.
The proud lords appear, appareled to ride.   1130
Leap lightly astride, lay hold of their bridles,
Each one on his way to his worthy house.
The liege lord of the land was not the last

Arrayed there to ride, with retainers many;
He had a bite to eat when he had heard mass;   1135
With horn to the hills he hastens amain.
By the dawn of that day over the dim earth,
Master and men were mounted and ready.
Then they harnessed in couples the keen-scented hounds,
Cast wide the kennel-door and called them forth,   1140
Blew upon their bugles bold blasts three;[16]
The dogs began to bay with a deafening din,
And they quieted them quickly and called them to heel,
A hundred brave huntsmen, as I have heard tell,
               together.   1145
       Men at stations meet;
       From the hounds they slip the tether;
       The echoing horns repeat,
       Clear in the merry weather.

At the clamor of the quest, the quarry trembled;   1150
Deer dashed through the dale, dazed with dread;
Hastened to the high ground, only to be
Turned back by the beaters, who boldly shouted.
They harmed not the harts, with their high heads,
Let the bucks go by, with their broad antlers,   1155
For it was counted a crime, in the close season,
If a man of that demesne should molest the male deer.
The hinds were headed up, with "Hey!" and "Ware!"
The does with great din were driven to the valleys.
Then you were ware, as they went, of the whistling of arrows; 1160
At each bend under boughs the bright shafts flew
That tore the tawny hide with their tapered heads.
Ah! they bray and they bleed, on banks they die,
And ever the pack pell-mell comes panting behind;
Hunters with shrill horns hot on their heels—   1165
Like the cracking of cliffs their cries resounded.
What game got away from the gallant archers
Was promptly picked off at the posts below
When they were harried on the heights and herded to the streams:
The watchers were so wary at the waiting-stations,   1170
And the greyhounds so huge, that eagerly snatched,
And finished them off as fast as folk could see
              with sight.
       The lord, now here, now there,
       Spurs forth in sheer delight.   1175

And drives, with pleasures rare,
The day to the dark night.

So the lord in the linden-wood leads the hunt
And Gawain the good knight in gay bed lies,
Lingered late alone, till daylight gleamed,   1180
Under coverlet costly, curtained about.
And as he slips into slumber, slyly there comes
A little din at his door, and the latch lifted,
And he holds up his heavy head out of the clothes;
A corner of the curtain he caught back a little   1185
And waited there warily, to see what befell.
Lo! it was the lady, loveliest to behold,
That drew the door behind her deftly and still
And was bound for his bed—abashed was the knight,
And laid his head low again in likeness of sleep;   1190
And she stepped stealthily, and stole to his bed,
Cast aside the curtain and came within,
And set herself softly on the bedside there,
And lingered at her leisure, to look on his waking.
The fair knight lay feigning for a long while,   1195
Conning in his conscience what his case might
Mean or amount to—a marvel he thought it.
But yet he said within himself, "More seemly it were
To try her intent by talking a little."
So he started and stretched, as startled from sleep,   1200
Lifts wide his lids in likeness of wonder,
And signs himself swiftly, as safer to be,
                    with art.
          Sweetly does she speak
          And kindling glances dart,   1205
          Blent white and red on cheek
          And laughing lips apart.

"Good morning, Sir Gawain," said that gay lady,
"A slack sleeper you are, to let one slip in!
Now you are taken in a trice—a truce we must make,   1210
Or I shall bind you in your bed, of that be assured."
Thus laughing lightly that lady jested.
"Good morning, good lady," said Gawain the blithe,
"Be it with me as you will; I am well content!
For I surrender myself, and sue for your grace,   1215
And that is best, I believe, and behooves me now."
Thus jested in answer that gentle knight.

"But if, lovely lady, you misliked it not,
And were pleased to permit your prisoner to rise,
I should quit this couch and accoutre me better,   1220
And be clad in more comfort for converse here."
"Nay, not so, sweet sir," said the smiling lady;
"You shall not rise from your bed; I direct you better:
I shall hem and hold you on either hand,
And keep company awhile with my captive knight.   1225
For as certain as I sit here, Sir Gawain you are,
Whom all the world worships, whereso you ride;
Your honor, your courtesy are highest acclaimed
By lords and by ladies, by all living men;
And lo! we are alone here, and left to ourselves;   1230
My lord and his liegemen are long departed,
The household asleep, my handmaids too,
The door drawn, and held by a well-driven bolt,
And since I have in this house him whom all love,
I shall while the time away with mirthful speech   1235
                          at will.
                  My body is here at hand,
                  Your each wish to fulfill;
                  Your servant to command
                  I am, and shall be still."[17]   1240

"In good faith," said Gawain, "my gain is the greater,
Though I am not he of whom you have heard;
To arrive at such reverence as you recount here
I am one all unworthy, and well do I know it.
By heaven, I would hold me the happiest of men   1245
If by word or by work I once might aspire
To the prize of your praise—'twere a pure joy!"
"In good faith, Sir Gawain," said that gay lady,
"The well-proven prowess that pleases all others,
Did I scant or scout it, 'twere scarce becoming.   1250
But there are ladies, believe me, that had liefer far
Have thee here in their hold, as I have today,
To pass an hour in pastime with pleasant words,
Assuage all their sorrows and solace their hearts,
Than much of the goodly gems and gold they possess.   1255
But laud be to the Lord of the lofty skies,
For here in my hands all hearts' desire
                          doth lie."
                  Great welcome got he there
                  From the lady who sat him by;   1260

> With fitting speech and fair
> The good knight makes reply.

"Madame," said the merry man, "Mary reward you!
For in good faith, I find your beneficence noble.
And the fame of fair deeds runs far and wide,   1265
But the praise you report pertains not to me,
But comes of your courtesy and kindness of heart."
"By the high Queen of heaven" (said she) "I count it not so,
For were I worth all the women in this world alive,
And all wealth and all worship were in my hands,   1270
And I should hunt high and low, a husband to take,
For the nurture I have noted in thee, knight, here,
The comeliness and courtesies and courtly mirth—
And so I had ever heard, and now hold it true—
No other on this earth, should have me for wife."   1275
"You are bound to a better man," the bold knight said,
"Yet I prize the praise you have proffered me here,
And soberly your servant, my sovereign I hold you,
And acknowledge me your knight, in the name of Christ."
So they talked of this and that until 'twas nigh noon,   1280
And ever the lady languishing in likeness of love.
With feat words and fair he framed his defense,
For were she never so winsome, the warrior had
The less will to woo, for the wound that his bane
                              must be.   1285
> He must bear the blinding blow,
> For such is fate's decree;
> The lady asks leave to go;
> He grants it full and free.

Then she gaily said goodbye, and glanced at him, laughing,   1290
And as she stood, she astonished him with a stern speech:
"Now may the Giver of all good words these glad hours repay!
But our guest is not Gawain—forgot is that thought."
"How so?" said the other, and asks in some haste,
For he feared he had been at fault in the forms of his speech.   1295
But she held up her hand, and made answer thus:
"So good a knight as Gawain is given out to be,
And the model of fair demeanor and manners pure,
Had he lain so long at a lady's side,
Would have claimed a kiss, by his courtesy,   1300
Through some touch or trick of phrase at some tale's end."
Said Gawain, "Good lady, I grant it at once!
I shall kiss at your command, as becomes a knight,

And more, lest you mislike, so let be, I pray."
With that she turns toward him, takes him in her arms,   1305
Leans down her lovely head, and lo! he is kissed.
They commend each other to Christ with comely words,
He sees her forth safely, in silence they part,
And then he lies no later in his lofty bed,
But calls to his chamberlain, chooses his clothes,   1310
Goes in those garments gladly to mass,
Then takes his way to table, where attendants wait,
And made merry all day, till the moon rose
                          in view
              Was never knight beset   1315
              'Twixt worthier ladies two:
              The crone and the coquette;
              Fair pastimes they pursue.

And the lord of the land rides late and long,
Hunting the barren hinds over the broad heath.   1320
He had slain such a sum, when the sun sank low,
Of does and other deer, as would dizzy one's wits.
Then they trooped in together in triumph at last,
And the count of the quarry quickly they take.
The lords lent a hand[18] with their liegemen many,   1325
Picked out the plumpest and put them together
And duly dressed the deer, as the deed requires.
Some were assigned the assay of the fat:
Two fingers'-width fully they found on the leanest.
Then they slit the slot open and searched out the paunch,   1330
Trimmed it with trencher-knives and tied it up tight.
They flayed the fair hide from the legs and trunk,
Then broke open the belly and laid bare the bowels,
Deftly detaching and drawing them forth.
And next at the neck they neatly parted   1335
The weasand from the windpipe, and cast away the guts.
At the shoulders with sharp blades they showed their skill,
Boning them from beneath, lest the sides be marred;
They breached the broad breast and broke it in twain,
And again at the gullet they begin with their knives,   1340
Cleave down the carcass clear to the breach;
Two tender morsels they take from the throat,
Then round the inner ribs they rid off a layer
And carve out the kidney-fat, close to the spine,
Hewing down to the haunch, that all hung together,   1345

And held it up whole, and hacked it free,
And this they named the numbles,[19] that knew such terms
                    of art.
            They divide the crotch in two,
            And straightway then they start   1350
            To cut the backbone through
            And cleave the trunk apart.

With hard strokes they hewed off the head and the neck,
Then swiftly from the sides they severed the chine,
And the corbie's bone they cast on a branch.[20]   1355
Then they pierced the plump sides, impaled either one
With the hock of the hind foot, and hung it aloft,
To each person his portion most proper and fit.
On a hide of a hind the hounds they fed
With the liver and the lights, the leathery paunches,   1360
And bread soaked in blood well blended therewith.
High horns and shrill set hounds a-baying,
Then merrily with their meat they make their way home,
Blowing on their bugles many a brave blast.
Ere dark had descended, that doughty band   1365
Was come within the walls where Gawain waits
                    at leisure.
            Bliss and hearth-fire bright
            Await the master's pleasure;
            When the two men met that night,   1370
            Joy surpassed all measure.

Then the host in the hall his household assembles,
With the dames of high degree and their damsels fair.
In the presence of the people, a party he sends
To convey him his venison in view of the knight.   1375
And in high good-humor he hails him then,
Counts over the kill, the cuts on the tallies,
Holds high the hewn ribs, heavy with fat.
"What think you, sir, of this? Have I thriven well?
Have I won with my woodcraft a worthy prize?"   1380
"In good earnest," said Gawain, "this game is the finest
I have seen in seven years in the season of winter."
"And I give it to you, Gawain," said the goodly host,
"For according to our covenant, you claim it as your own."
"That is so," said Sir Gawain, "the same say I: 1385
What I worthily have won within these fair walls,
Herewith I as willingly award it to you."

He embraces his broad neck with both his arms,
And confers on him a kiss in the comeliest style.
"Have here my profit, it proved no better;   1390
Ungrudging do I grant it, were it greater far."
"Such a gift," said the good host, "I gladly accept—
Yet it might be all the better, would you but say
Where you won this same award, by your wits alone."
"That was no part of the pact; press me no further,   1395
For you have had what behooves; all other claims
                              forbear."
                    With jest and compliment
                    They conversed, and cast off care;
                    To the table soon they went;   1400
                    Fresh dainties wait them there.

And then by the chimney-side they chat at their ease;
The best wine was brought them, and bounteously served;
And after in their jesting they jointly accord
To do on the second day the deeds of the first: 1405
That the two men should trade, betide as it may,
What each had taken in, at eve when they met.
They seal the pact solemnly in sight of the court;
Their cups were filled afresh to confirm the jest;
Then at last they took their leave, for late was the hour,   1410
Each to his own bed hastening away.
Before the barnyard cock had crowed but thrice
The lord had leapt from his rest, his liegemen as well.
Both of mass and their meal they made short work:
By the dim light of dawn they were deep in the woods   1415
                              away.
                    With huntsmen and with horns
                    Over plains they pass that day;
                    They release, amid the thorns,
                    Swift hounds that run and bay.   1420

Soon some were on a scent by the side of a marsh;
When the hounds opened cry, the head of the hunt
Rallied them with rough words, raised a great noise.
The hounds that had heard it came hurrying straight
And followed along with their fellows, forty together.   1425
Then such a clamor and cry of coursing hounds
Arose, that the rocks resounded again.
Hunters exhorted them with horn and with voice;
Then all in a body bore off together
Between a mere in the marsh and a menacing crag,   1430

To a rise where the rock stood rugged and steep,
And boulders lay about, that blocked their approach.
Then the company in consort closed on their prey:
They surrounded the rise and the rocks both,
For well they were aware that it waited within,   1435
The beast that the bloodhounds boldly proclaimed.
Then they beat on the bushes and bade him appear,
And he made a murderous rush in the midst of them all;
The best of all boars broke from his cover,
That had ranged long unrivaled, a renegade old,   1440
For of tough-brawned boars he was biggest far,
Most grim when he grunted—then grieved were many,
For three at the first thrust he threw to the earth,
And dashed away at once without more damage.
With "Hi!" "Hi!" and "Hey!" "Hey!" the others followed,   1445
Had horns at their lips, blew high and clear.
Merry was the music of men and of hounds
That were bound after this boar, his bloodthirsty heart
                         to quell.
               Often he stands at bay,   1450
               Then scatters the pack pell-mell;
               He hurts the hounds, and they
               Most dolefully yowl and yell.

Men then with mighty bows moved in to shoot,
Aimed at him with their arrows and often hit,   1455
But the points had no power to pierce through his hide,
And the barbs were brushed aside by his bristly brow;
Though the shank of the shaft shivered in pieces,
The head hopped away, wheresoever it struck.
But when their stubborn strokes had stung him at last,   1460
Then, foaming in his frenzy, fiercely he charges,
Hies at them headlong that hindered his flight,
And many feared for their lives, and fell back a little.
But the lord on a lively horse leads the chase;
As a high-mettled huntsman his horn he blows;   1465
He sounds the assembly and sweeps through the brush,
Pursuing this wild swine till the sunlight slanted.
All day with this deed they drive forth the time
While our lone knight so lovesome lies in his bed,
Sir Gawain safe at home, in silken bower   1470
                    so gay,
               The lady, with guile in heart,
               Came early where he lay;

She was at him with all her art
To turn his mind her way.   1475

She comes to the curtain and coyly peeps in;
Gawain thought it good to greet her at once,
And she richly repays him with her ready words,
Settles softly at his side, and suddenly she laughs,
And with a gracious glance, she begins on him thus: 1480
"Sir, if you be Gawain, it seems a great wonder—
A man so well-meaning, and mannerly disposed,
And cannot act in company as courtesy bids,
And if one takes the trouble to teach him, 'tis all in vain.
That lesson learned lately is lightly forgot,   1485
Though I painted it as plain as my poor wit allowed."
"What lesson, dear lady?" he asked all alarmed;
"I have been much to blame, if your story be true."
"Yet my counsel was of kissing," came her answer then,
"Where favor has been found, freely to claim   1490
As accords with the conduct of courteous knights."
"My dear," said the doughty man, "dismiss that thought;
Such freedom, I fear, might offend you much;
It were rude to request if the right were denied."
"But none can deny you," said the noble dame,   1495
"You are stout enough to constrain with strength, if you choose,
Were any so ungracious as to grudge you aught."
"By heaven," said he, "you have answered well,
But threats never throve among those of my land,
Nor any gift not freely given, good though it be.   1500
I am yours to command, to kiss when you please;
You may lay on as you like, and leave off at will."

With this,
The lady lightly bends
And graciously gives him a kiss;   1505
The two converse as friends
Of true love's trials and bliss.

"I should like, by your leave," said the lovely lady,
"If it did not annoy you, to know for what cause
So brisk and so bold a young blood as you,   1510
And acclaimed for all courtesies becoming a knight—
And name what knight you will, they are noblest esteemed
For loyal faith in love, in life as in story;
For to tell the tribulations of these true hearts,
Why, 'tis the very title and text of their deeds,   1515
How bold knights for beauty have braved many a foe,

Suffered heavy sorrows out of secret love,
And then valorously avenged them on villainous churls
And made happy ever after the hearts of their ladies.
And you are the noblest knight known in your time;   1520
No household under heaven but has heard of your fame,
And here by your side I have sat for two days
Yet never has a fair phrase fallen from your lips
Of the language of love, not one little word!
And you, that with sweet vows sway women's hearts,   1525
Should show your winsome ways, and woo a young thing,
And teach by some tokens the craft of true love.
How! are you artless, whom all men praise?
Or do you deem me so dull, or deaf to such words?
                            Fie! Fie!   1530
                    In hope of pastimes new
                    I have come where none can spy;
                    Instruct me a little, do,
                    While my husband is not nearby."

"God love you, gracious lady!" said Gawain then;   1535
"It is a pleasure surpassing, and a peerless joy,
That one so worthy as you would willingly come
And take the time and trouble to talk with your knight
And content you with his company—it comforts my heart.
But to take to myself the task of telling of love,   1540
And touch upon its texts, and treat of its themes
To one that, I know well, wields more power
In that art, by a half, than a hundred such
As I am where I live, or am like to become,
It were folly, fair dame, in the first degree!   1545
In all that I am able, my aim is to please,
As in honor behooves me, and am evermore
Your servant heart and soul, so save me our Lord!"
Thus she tested his temper and tried many a time,
Whatever her true intent, to entice him to sin,   1550
But so fair was his defense that no fault appeared,
Nor evil on either hand, but only bliss
                            they knew.
                    They linger and laugh awhile;
                    She kisses the knight so true,   1555
                    Takes leave in comeliest style
                    And departs without more ado.

Then he rose from his rest and made ready for mass,
And then a meal was set and served, in sumptuous style;

He dallied at home all day with the dear ladies,   1560
But the lord lingered late at his lusty sport;
Pursued his sorry swine, that swerved as he fled,
And bit asunder the backs of the best of his hounds
When they brought him to bay, till the bowmen appeared
And soon forced him forth, though he fought for dear life,   1565
So sharp were the shafts they shot at him there.
But yet the boldest drew back from his battering head,
Till at last he was so tired he could travel no more,
But in as much haste as he might, he makes his retreat
To a rise on rocky ground, by a rushing stream.   1570
With the bank at his back he scrapes the bare earth,
The froth foams at his jaws, frightful to see.
He whets his white tusks—then weary were all
Those hunters so hardy that hoved round about
Of aiming from afar, but ever they mistrust   1575
                    his mood.
            He had hurt so many by then
            That none had hardihood
            To be torn by his tusks again,
            That was brainsick, and out for blood.   1580

Till the lord came at last on his lofty steed,
Beheld him there at bay before all his folk;
Lightly he leaps down, leaves his courser,
Bares his bright sword, and boldly advances;
Straight into the stream he strides towards his foe.   1585
The wild thing was wary of weapon and man;
His hackles rose high; so hotly he snorts
That many watched with alarm, lest the worst befall.
The boar makes for the man with a mighty bound
So that he and his hunter came headlong together   1590
Where the water ran wildest—the worse for the beast,
For the man, when they first met, marked him with care,
Sights well the slot, slips in the blade,
Shoves it home to the hilt, and the heart shattered,
And he falls in his fury and floats down the water,   1595
                    ill-sped.
            Hounds hasten by the score
            To maul him, hide and head;
            Men drag him in to shore
            And dogs pronounce him dead.   1600

With many a brave blast they boast of their prize,
All hallooed in high glee, that had their wind;

The hounds bayed their best, as the bold men bade
That were charged with chief rank in that chase of renown.
Then one wise in woodcraft, and worthily skilled,   1605
Began to dress the boar in becoming style:
He severs the savage head and sets it aloft,
Then rends the body roughly right down the spine;
Takes the bowels from the belly, broils them on coals,
Blends them well with bread to bestow on the hounds.   1610
Then he breaks out the brawn in fair broad flitches,
And the innards to be eaten in order he takes.
The two sides, attached to each other all whole,
He suspended from a spar that was springy and tough;
And so with this swine they set out for home;   1615
The boar's head was borne before the same man
That had stabbed him in the stream with his strong arm,
     right through.
    He thought it long indeed
    Till he had the knight in view;
    At his call, he comes with speed   1620
    To claim his payment due.

The lord laughed aloud, with many a light word,
When he greeted Sir Gawain—with good cheer he speaks.
They fetch the fair dames and the folk of the house;   1625
He brings forth the brawn, and begins the tale
Of the great length and girth, the grim rage as well,
Of the battle of the boar they beset in the wood.
The other man meetly commended his deeds
And praised well the prize of his princely sport,   1630
For the brawn of that boar, the bold knight said,
And the sides of that swine surpassed all others.
Then they handled the huge head; he owns it a wonder,
And eyes it with abhorrence, to heighten his praise.
"Now, Gawain," said the good man, "this game becomes yours   1635
By those fair terms we fixed, as you know full well."
"That is true," returned the knight, "and trust me, fair friend,
All my gains, as agreed, I shall give you forthwith."
He clasps him and kisses him in courteous style,
Then serves him with the same fare a second time.   1640
"Now we are even," said he, "at this evening feast,
And clear is every claim incurred here to date,
     and debt."
    "By Saint Giles!" the host replies,
    "You're the best I ever met!   1645

If your profits are all this size,
We'll see you wealthy yet!"

Then attendants set tables on trestles about,
And laid them with linen; light shone forth,
Wakened along the walls in waxen torches.   1650
The service was set and the supper brought;
Royal were the revels that rose then in hall
At that feast by the fire, with many fair sports:
Amid the meal and after, melody sweet,
Carol-dances comely and Christmas songs,   1655
With all the mannerly mirth my tongue may describe.
And ever our gallant knight beside the gay lady;
So uncommonly kind and complaisant was she,
With sweet stolen glances, that stirred his stout heart,
That he was at his wits' end, and wondrous vexed;   1660
But he could not in conscience her courtship repay,
Yet took pains to please her, though the plan might
                    go wrong.
            When they to heart's delight
            Had reveled there in throng,   1665
            To his chamber he calls the knight,
            And thither they go along.

And there they dallied and drank, and deemed it good sport
To enact their play anew on New Year's Eve,
But Gawain asked again to go on the morrow,   1670
For the time until his tryst was not two days.
The host hindered that, and urged him to stay,
And said, "On my honor, my oath here I take
That you shall get to the Green Chapel to begin your chores
By dawn on New Year's Day, if you so desire.   1675
Wherefore lie at your leisure in your lofty bed,
And I shall hunt hereabouts, and hold to our terms,
And we shall trade winnings when once more we meet,
For I have tested you twice, and true have I found you;
Now think this tomorrow: the third pays for all;   1680
Be we merry while we may, and mindful of joy,
For heaviness of heart can be had for the asking."
This is gravely agreed on and Gawain will stay.
They drink a last draught and with torches depart
                    to rest.   1685
            To bed Sir Gawain went;
            His sleep was of the best;

The lord, on his craft intent,
Was early up and dressed.

After mass, with his men, a morsel he takes;   1690
Clear and crisp the morning; he calls for his mount;
The folk that were to follow him afield that day
Were high astride their horses before the hall gates.
Wondrous fair were the fields, for the frost was light;
The sun rises red amid radiant clouds,   1695
Sails into the sky, and sends forth his beams.
They let loose the hounds by a leafy wood;
The rocks all around re-echo to their horns;
Soon some have set off in pursuit of the fox,
Cast about with craft for a clearer scent;   1700
A young dog yaps, and is yelled at in turn;
His fellows fall to sniffing, and follow his lead,
Running in a rabble on the right track,
And he scampers all before; they discover him soon,
And when they see him with sight they pursue him the faster,   1705
Railing at him rudely with a wrathful din.
Often he reverses over rough terrain,
Or loops back to listen in the lee of a hedge;
At last, by a little ditch, he leaps over the brush,
Comes into a clearing at a cautious pace,   1710
Then he thought through his wiles to have thrown off the hounds
Till he was ware, as he went, of a waiting-station
Where three athwart his path threatened him at once,
                    all gray.
                    Quick as a flash he wheels   1715
                    And darts off in dismay;
                    With hard luck at his heels
                    He is off to the wood away.

Then it was heaven on earth to hark to the hounds
When they had come on their quarry, coursing together!   1720
Such harsh cries and howls they hurled at his head
As all the cliffs with a crash had come down at once.
Here he was hailed, when huntsmen met him;
Yonder they yelled at him, yapping and snarling;
There they cried "Thief!" and threatened his life,   1725
And ever the harriers at his heels, that he had no rest.
Often he was menaced when he made for the open,
And often rushed in again, for Reynard was wily;
And so he leads them a merry chase, the lord and his men,

In this manner on the mountains, till midday or near,   1730
While our hero lies at home in wholesome sleep
Within the comely curtains on the cold morning.
But the lady, as love would allow her no rest,
And pursuing ever the purpose that pricked her heart,
Was awake with the dawn, and went to his chamber   1735
In a fair flowing mantle that fell to the earth,
All edged and embellished with ermines fine;
No hood on her head, but heavy with gems
Were her fillet and the fret that confined her tresses;
Her face and her fair throat freely displayed;   1740
Her bosom all but bare, and her back as well.
She comes in at the chamber-door, and closes it with care,
Throws wide a window—then waits no longer,
But hails him thus airily with her artful words,
                  with cheer: 1745
        "Ah, man, how can you sleep?
        The morning is so clear!"
        Though dreams have drowned him deep,
        He cannot choose but hear.

Deep in his dreams he darkly mutters   1750
As a man may that mourns, with many grim thoughts
Of that day when destiny shall deal him his doom
When he greets his grim host at the Green Chapel
And must bow to his buffet, bating all strife.
But when he sees her at his side he summons his wits,   1755
Breaks from the black dreams, and blithely answers.
That lovely lady comes laughing sweet,
Sinks down at his side, and salutes him with a kiss.
He accords her fair welcome in courtliest style;
He sees her so glorious, so gaily attired,   1760
So faultless her features, so fair and so bright,
His heart swelled swiftly with surging joys.
They melt into mirth with many a fond smile,
And there was bliss beyond telling between those two,
                  at height.   1765
        Good were their words of greeting;
        Each joyed in other's sight;
        Great peril attends that meeting
        Should Mary forget her knight.

For that high-born beauty so hemmed him about,   1770
Made so plain her meaning, the man must needs
Either take her tendered love or distastefully refuse.

His courtesy concerned him, lest crass he appear,
But more his soul's mischief, should he commit sin
And belie his loyal oath to the lord of that house.   1775
"God forbid!" said the bold knight, "That shall not befall!"
With a little fond laughter he lightly let pass
All the words of special weight that were sped his way;
"I find you much at fault," the fair one said,
"Who can be cold toward a creature so close by your side,   1780
Of all women in this world most wounded in heart,
Unless you have a sweetheart, one you hold dearer,
And allegiance to that lady so loyally knit
That you will never love another, as now I believe.
And, sir, if it be so, then say it, I beg you;   1785
By all your heart holds dear, hide it no longer
                        with guile."
                "Lady, by Saint John,"
                He answers with a smile,
                "Lover have I none,   1790
                Nor will have, yet awhile."

"Those words," said the woman, "are the worst of all,
But I have had my answer, and hard do I find it!
Kiss me now kindly; I can but go hence
To lament my life long like a maid lovelorn."   1795
She inclines her head quickly and kisses the knight,
Then straightens with a sigh, and says as she stands,
"Now, dear, ere I depart, do me this pleasure:
Give me some little gift, your glove or the like,
That I may think on you, man, and mourn the less."   1800
"Now by heaven," said he, "I wish I had here
My most precious possession, to put it in your hands,
For your deeds, beyond doubt, have often deserved
A repayment far passing my power to bestow.
But a love-token, lady, were of little avail;   1805
It is not to your honor to have at this time
A glove as a guerdon from Gawain's hand,
And I am here on an errand in unknown realms
And have no bearers with baggage with becoming gifts,
Which distresses me, madame, for your dear sake.   1810
A man must keep within his compass: account it neither grief
                        nor slight."
                "Nay, noblest knight alive,"
                Said that beauty of body white,
                "Though you be loath to give,   1815
                Yet you shall take, by right."

She reached out a rich ring, wrought all of gold,
With a splendid stone displayed on the band
That flashed before his eyes like a fiery sun;
It was worth a king's wealth, you may well believe.   1820
But he waved it away with these ready words:
"Before God, good lady, I forego all gifts;
None have I to offer, nor any will I take."
And she urged it on him eagerly, and ever he refused,
And vowed in very earnest, prevail she would not.   1825
And she sad to find it so, and said to him then,
"If my ring is refused for its rich cost—
You would not be my debtor for so dear a thing—
I shall give you my girdle; you gain less thereby."
She released a knot lightly, and loosened a belt   1830
That was caught about her kirtle, the bright cloak beneath,
Of a gay green silk, with gold overwrought,
And the borders all bound with embroidery fine,
And this she presses upon him, and pleads with a smile,
Unworthy though it were, that it would not be scorned.   1835
But the man still maintains that he means to accept
Neither gold nor any gift, till by God's grace
The fate that lay before him was fully achieved.
"And be not offended, fair lady, I beg,
And give over your offer, for ever I must   1840
                         decline.
              I am grateful for favor shown
              Past all deserts of mine,
              And ever shall be your own
              True servant, rain or shine."   1845

"Now does my present displease you," she promptly inquired,
"Because it seems in your sight so simple a thing?
And belike, as it is little, it is less to praise,
But if the virtue that invests it were verily known,
It would be held, I hope, in higher esteem.   1850
For the man that possesses this piece of silk,
If he bore it on his body, belted about,
There is no hand under heaven that could hew him down,
For he could not be killed by any craft on earth."
Then the man began to muse, and mainly he thought   1855
It was a pearl for his plight, the peril to come
When he gains the Green Chapel to get his reward:
Could he escape unscathed, the scheme were noble!
Then he bore with her words and withstood them no more,

And she repeated her petition and pleaded anew, 1860
And he granted it, and gladly she gave him the belt,
And besought him for her sake to conceal it well,
Lest the noble lord should know—and the knight agrees
That not a soul save themselves shall see it thenceforth
                         with sight. 1865
             He thanked her with fervent heart,
             As often as ever he might;
             Three times, before they part,
             She has kissed the stalwart knight.

Then the lady took her leave, and left him there, 1870
For more mirth with that man she might not have.
When she was gone, Sir Gawain got from his bed,
Arose and arrayed him in his rich attire;
Tucked away the token the temptress had left,
Laid it reliably where he looked for it after. 1875
And then with good cheer to the chapel he goes,
Approached a priest in private, and prayed to be taught
To lead a better life and lift up his mind,
Lest he be among the lost when he must leave this world.
And shamefaced at shrift he showed his misdeeds 1880
From the largest to the least, and asked the Lord's mercy,[21]
And called on his confessor to cleanse his soul,
And he absolved him of his sins as safe and as clean
As if the dread Day of Judgment should dawn on the morrow.
And then he made merry amid the fine ladies 1885
With deft-footed dances and dalliance light,
As never until now, while the afternoon wore
                   away.
             He delighted all around him,
             And all agreed, that day, 1890
             They never before had found him
             So gracious and so gay.

Now peaceful be his pasture, and love play him fair!
The host is on horseback, hunting afield;
He has finished off this fox that he followed so long: 1895
As he leapt a low hedge to look for the villain
Where he heard all the hounds in hot pursuit,
Reynard comes racing out of a rough thicket,
And all the rabble in a rush, right at his heels.
The man beholds the beast, and bides his time, 1900
And bares his bright sword, and brings it down hard,
And he blenches from the blade, and backward he starts;

A hound hurries up and hinders that move,
And before the horse's feet they fell on him at once
And ripped the rascal's throat with a wrathful din.   1905
The lord soon alighted and lifted him free,
Swiftly snatched him up from the snapping jaws,
Holds him over his head, halloos with a will,
And the dogs bayed the dirge, that had done him to death.
Hunters hastened thither with horns at their lips,   1910
Sounding the assembly till they saw him at last.
When that comely company was come in together,
All that bore bugles blew them at once,
And the others all hallooed, that had no horns.
It was the merriest medley that ever a man heard,   1915
The racket that they raised for Sir Reynard's soul
                  that died.
          Their hounds they praised and fed,
          Fondling their heads with pride,
          And they took Reynard the Red   1920
          And stripped away his hide.

And then they headed homeward, for evening had come,
Blowing many a blast on their bugles bright.
The lord at long last alights at his house,
Finds fire on the hearth where the fair knight waits,   1925
Sir Gawain the good, that was glad in heart.
With the ladies, that loved him, he lingered at ease;
He wore a rich robe of blue, that reached to the earth
And a surcoat lined softly with sumptuous furs;
A hood of the same hue hung on his shoulders;   1930
With bands of bright ermine embellished were both.
He comes to meet the man amid all the folk,
And greets him good-humoredly, and gaily he says,
"I shall follow forthwith the form of our pledge
That we framed to good effect amid fresh-filled cups."   1935
He clasps him accordingly and kisses him thrice,
As amiably and as earnestly as ever he could.
"By heaven," said the host, "you have had some luck
Since you took up this trade, if the terms were good."
"Never trouble about the terms," he returned at once,   1940
"Since all that I owe here is openly paid."
"Marry!" said the other man, "mine is much less,
For I have hunted all day, and nought have I got
But this foul fox pelt, the fiend take the goods!

Which but poorly repays those precious things   1945
That you have cordially conferred, those kisses three
                so good."
           "Enough!" said Sir Gawain;
           "I thank you, by the rood!"
           And how the fox was slain   1950
           He told him, as they stood.

With minstrelsy and mirth, with all manner of meats,
They made as much merriment as any men might
(Amid laughing of ladies and light-hearted girls,
So gay grew Sir Gawain and the goodly host)   1955
Unless they had been besotted, or brainless fools.
The knight joined in jesting with that joyous folk,
Until at last it was late; ere long they must part,
And be off to their beds, as behooved them each one.
Then politely his leave of the lord of the house   1960
Our noble knight takes, and renews his thanks:
"The courtesies countless accorded me here,
Your kindness at this Christmas, may heaven's King repay!
Henceforth, if you will have me, I hold you my liege,
And so, as I have said, I must set forth tomorrow,   1965
If I may take some trusty man to teach, as you promised,
The way to the Green Chapel, that as God allows
I shall see my fate fulfilled on the first of the year."
"In good faith," said the good man, "with a good will
Every promise on my part shall be fully performed."   1970
He assigns him a servant to set him on the path,
To see him safe and sound over the snowy hills,
To follow the fastest way through forest green
               and grove.
           Gawain thanks him again.   1975
           So kind his favors prove,
           And of the ladies then
           He takes his leave, with love.

Courteously he kissed them, with care in his heart,
And often wished them well, with warmest thanks,   1980
Which they for their part were prompt to repay.
They commend him to Christ with disconsolate sighs;
And then in that hall with the household he parts—
Each man that he met, he remembered to thank
For his deeds of devotion and diligent pains,   1985
And the trouble he had taken to tend to his needs;

And each one as woeful, that watched him depart,
As he had lived with him loyally all his life long.
By lads bearing lights he was led to his chamber
And blithely brought to his bed, to be at his rest.   1990
How soundly he slept, I presume not to say,
For there were matters of moment his thoughts might well
                              pursue.
                    Let him lie and wait;
                    He has little more to do,   1995
                    Then listen, while I relate
                    How they kept their rendezvous.

Part IV

Now the New Year draws hear, and the night passes,
The day dispels the dark, by the Lord's decree;
But wild weather awoke in the world without: 2000
The clouds in the cold sky cast down their snow
With great gusts from the north, grievous to bear.
Sleet showered aslant upon shivering beasts;
The wind warbled wild as it whipped from aloft,
And drove the drifts deep in the dales below.   2005
Long and well he listens, that lies in his bed;
Though he lifts not his eyelids, little he sleeps;
Each crow of the cock he counts without fail.
Readily from his rest he rose before dawn,
For a lamp had been left him, that lighted his chamber.   2010
He called to his chamberlain, who quickly appeared,
And bade him get him his gear, and gird his good steed,
And he sets about briskly to bring in his arms,
And makes ready his master in manner most fit.
First he clad him in his clothes, to keep out the cold,   2015
And then his other harness, made handsome anew,
His plate-armor of proof, polished with pains,
The rings of his rich mail rid of their rust,
And all was fresh as at first, and for this he gave thanks
                              indeed.   2020
                    With pride he wears each piece,
                    New-furbished for his need:
                    No gayer from here to Greece;
                    He bids them bring his steed.

In his richest raiment he robed himself then: 2025
His crested coat-armor, close-stitched with craft,

With stones of strange virtue on silk velvet set;
All bound with embroidery on borders and seams
And lined warmly and well with furs of the best.
Yet he left not his love-gift, the lady's girdle;   2030
Gawain, for his own good, forgot not that:
When the bright sword was belted and bound on his haunches,
Then twice with that token he twined him about.
Sweetly did he swathe him in that swatch of silk,
That girdle of green so goodly to see,   2035
That against the gay red showed gorgeous bright.
Yet he wore not for its wealth that wondrous girdle,
Nor pride in its pendants, though polished they were,
Though glittering gold gleamed at the ends,
But to keep himself safe when consent he must   2040
To endure a deadly dint, and all defense
                         denied.
              And now the bold knight came
              Into the courtyard wide;
              That folk of worthy fame   2045
              He thanks on every side.

Then was Gringolet girt, that was great and huge,
And had sojourned safe and sound, and savored his fare;
He pawed the earth in his pride, that princely steed.
The good knight draws near him and notes well his look,   2050
And says sagely to himself, and soberly swears,
"Here is a household in hall that upholds the right!
The man that maintains it, may happiness be his!
Likewise the dear lady, may love betide her!
If thus they in charity cherish a guest   2055
That are honored here on earth, may they have His reward
That reigns high in heaven—and also you all;
And were I to live in this land but a little while,
I should willingly reward you, and well, if I might."
Then he steps into the stirrup and bestrides his mount;   2060
His shield is shown forth; on his shoulder he casts it;
Strikes the side of his steed with his steel spurs,
And he starts across the stones, nor stands any longer
                         to prance.
              On horseback was the swain   2065
              That bore his spear and lance;
              "May Christ this house maintain
              And guard it from mischance!"

The bridge was brought down, and the broad gates
Unbarred and carried back upon both sides;   2070
He commended him to Christ, and crossed over the planks;
Praised the noble porter, who prayed on his knees
That God save Sir Gawain, and bade him good day,
And went on his way alone with the man
That was to lead him ere long to that luckless place   2075
Where the dolorous dint must be dealt him at last.
Under bare boughs they ride, where steep banks rise,
Over high cliffs they climb, where cold snow clings;
The heavens held aloof, but heavy thereunder
Mist mantled the moors, moved on the slopes.   2080
Each hill had a hat, a huge cape of cloud;
Brooks bubbled and broke over broken rocks,
Flashing in freshets that waterfalls fed.
Roundabout was the road that ran through the wood
Till the sun at that season was soon to rise,   2085
                that day.
            They were on a hilltop high;
            The white snow round them lay;
            The man that rode nearby
            Now bade his master stay.   2090

"For I have seen you here safe at the set time,
And now you are not far from that notable place
That you have sought for so long with such special pains.
But this I say for certain, since I know you, sir knight,
And have your good at heart, and hold you dear—   2095
Would you heed well my words, it were worth your while—
You are rushing into risks that you reck not of:
There is a villain in yon valley, the veriest on earth,
For he is rugged and rude, and ready with his fists,
And most immense in his mold of mortals alive,   2100
And his body bigger than the best four
That are in Arthur's house, Hector or any.
He gets his grim way at the Green Chapel;
None passes by that place so proud in his arms
That he does not dash him down with his deadly blows,   2105
For he is heartless wholly, and heedless of right,
For be it chaplain or churl that by the Chapel rides,
Monk or mass-priest or any man else,
He would as soon strike him dead as stand on two feet.
Wherefore I say, just as certain as you sit there astride,   2110

You cannot but be killed, if his counsel holds,
For he would trounce you in a trice, had you twenty lives
                          for sale.
              He has lived long in this land
              And dealt out deadly bale;   2115
              Against his heavy hand
              Your power cannot prevail.

"And so, good Sir Gawain, let the grim man be;
Go off by some other road, in God's own name!
Leave by some other land, for the love of Christ,   2120
And I shall get me home again, and give you my word
That I shall swear by God's self and the saints above,
By heaven and by my halidom and other oaths more,
To conceal this day's deed, nor say to a soul
That ever you fled for fear from any that I knew."   2125
"Many thanks!" said the other man—and demurring he speaks—
"Fair fortune befall you for your friendly words!
And conceal this day's deed I doubt not you would,
But though you never told the tale, if I turned back now,
Forsook this place for fear, and fled, as you say,   2130
I were a caitiff coward; I could not be excused.
But I must to the Chapel to chance my luck
And say to that same man such words as I please,
Befall what may befall through Fortune's will
                          or whim.   2135
              Though he be a quarrelsome knave
              With a cudgel great and grim,
              The Lord is strong to save:
              His servants trust in Him."

"Marry," said the man, "since you tell me so much,   2140
And I see you are set to seek your own harm,
If you crave a quick death, let me keep you no longer!
Put your helm on your head, your hand on your lance,
And ride the narrow road down yon rocky slope
Till it brings you to the bottom of the broad valley.   2145
Then look a little ahead, on your left hand,
And you will soon see before you that self-same Chapel,
And the man of great might that is master there.
Now goodbye in God's name, Gawain the noble!
For all the world's wealth I would not stay here,   2150
Or go with you in this wood one footstep further!"
He tarried no more to talk, but turned his bridle,

Hit his horse with his heels as hard as he might,
Leaves the knight alone, and off like the wind
                 goes leaping.   2155
            "By God," said Gawain then,
            "I shall not give way to weeping;
            God's will be done, amen!
            I commend me to His keeping."

He puts his heels to his horse, and picks up the path;   2160
Goes in beside a grove where the ground is steep,
Rides down the rough slope right to the valley;
And then he looked a little about him—the landscape was wild,
And not a soul to be seen, nor sign of a dwelling,
But high banks on either hand hemmed it about,   2165
With many a ragged rock and rough-hewn crag;
The skies seemed scored by the scowling peaks.
Then he halted his horse, and hoved there a space,
And sought on every side for a sight of the Chapel,
But no such place appeared, which puzzled him sore,   2170
Yet he saw some way off what seemed like a mound,
A hillock high and broad, hard by the water,
Where the stream fell in foam down the face of the steep
And bubbled as if it boiled on its bed below.
The knight urges his horse, and heads for the knoll;   2175
Leaps lightly to earth; loops well the rein
Of his steed to a stout branch, and stations him there.
He strides straight to the mound, and strolls all about,
Much wondering what it was, but no whit the wiser;
It had a hole at one end, and on either side,   2180
And was covered with coarse grass in clumps all without,
And hollow all within, like some old cave,
Or a crevice of an old crag—he could not discern
                 aright.
            "Can this be the Chapel Green?   2185
            Alack!" said the man, "Here might
            The devil himself be seen
            Saying matins at black midnight!"

"Now by heaven," said he, "it is bleak hereabouts;
This prayer-house is hideous, half-covered with grass!   2190
Well may the grim man mantled in green
Hold here his orisons, in hell's own style!
Now I feel it is the Fiend, in my five wits,
That has tempted me to this tryst, to take my life;
This is a Chapel of mischance, may the mischief take it!   2195

As accursed a country church as I came upon ever!"
With his helm on his head, his lance in his hand,
He stalks toward the steep wall of that strange house.
Then he heard, on the hill, behind a hard rock,
Beyond the brook, from the bank, a most barbarous din: 2200
Lord! it clattered in the cliff fit to cleave it in two,
As one upon a grindstone ground a great scythe!
Lord! it whirred like a mill-wheel whirling about!
Lord! it echoed loud and long, lamentable to hear!
Then "By heaven," said the bold knight, "That business up there   2205
Is arranged for my arrival, or else I am much
                              misled.
                  Let God work! Ah me!
                  All hope of help has fled!
                  Forfeit my life may be   2210
                  But noise I do not dread."

Then he listened no longer, but loudly he called,
"Who has power in this place, high parley to hold?
For none greets Sir Gawain, or gives him good day;
If any would a word with him, let him walk forth   2215
And speak now or never, to speed his affairs."
"Abide," said one on the bank above over his head,
"And what I promised you once shall straightway be given."
Yet he stayed not his grindstone, nor stinted its noise,
But worked awhile at his whetting before he would rest,   2220
And then he comes around a crag, from a cave in the rocks,
Hurtling out of hiding with a hateful weapon,
A Danish ax devised for that day's deed,
With a broad blade and bright, bent in a curve,
Filed to a fine edge—four feet it measured   2225
By the length of the lace that was looped round the haft.
And in form as at first, the fellow all green,
His lordly face and his legs, his locks and his beard,
Save that firm upon two feet forward he strides,
Sets a hand on the ax-head, the haft to the earth;   2230
When he came to the cold stream, and cared not to wade,
He vaults over on his ax, and advances amain
On a broad bank of snow, overbearing and brisk
                              of mood.
                  Little did the knight incline   2235
                  When face to face they stood;
                  Said the other man, "Friend mine,
                  It seems your word holds good!"

"God love you, Sir Gawain!" said the Green Knight then,
"And well met this morning, man, at my place!   2240
And you have followed me faithfully and found me betimes,
And on the business between us we both are agreed:
Twelve months ago today you took what was yours,
And you at this New Year must yield me the same.
And we have met in these mountains, remote from all eyes: 2245
There is none here to halt us or hinder our sport;
Unhasp your high helm, and have here your wages;
Make no more demur than I did myself
When you hacked off my head with one hard blow."
"No, by God," said Sir Gawain, "that granted me life,   2250
I shall grudge not the guerdon, grim though it prove;
Bestow but one stroke, and I shall stand still,
And you may lay on as you like till the last of my part
                          be paid."
                    He proffered, with good grace,   2255
                    His bare neck to the blade,
                    And feigned a cheerful face:
                    He scorned to seem afraid.

Then the grim man in green gathers his strength,
Heaves high the heavy ax to hit him the blow.   2260
With all the force in his frame he fetches it aloft,
With a grimace as grim as he would grind him to bits;
Had the blow he bestowed been as big as he threatened,
A good knight and gallant had gone to his grave.
But Gawain at the great ax glanced up aside   2265
As down it descended with death-dealing force,
And his shoulders shrank a little from the sharp iron.
Abruptly the brawny man breaks off the stroke,
And then reproved with proud words that prince among knights.
"You are not Gawain the glorious," the green man said,   2270
"That never fell back on field in the face of the foe,
And now you flee for fear, and have felt no harm:
Such news of that knight I never heard yet!
I moved not a muscle when you made to strike,
Nor caviled at the cut in King Arthur's house;   2275
My head fell to my feet, yet steadfast I stood,
And you, all unharmed, are wholly dismayed—
Wherefore the better man I, by all odds,
                          must be."
                    Said Gawain, "Strike once more;   2280
                    I shall neither flinch nor flee;

> But if my head falls to the floor
> There is no mending me!"

"But go on, man, in God's name, and get to the point!
Deliver me my destiny, and do it out of hand,　　　　　　2285
For I shall stand to the stroke and stir not an inch
Till your ax has hit home—on my honor I swear it!"
"Have at thee then!" said the other, and heaves it aloft,
And glares down as grimly as he had gone mad.
He made a mighty feint, but marred not his hide;　　　　2290
Withdrew the ax adroitly before it did damage.
Gawain gave no ground, nor glanced up aside,
But stood still as a stone, or else a stout stump
That is held in hard earth by a hundred roots.
Then merrily does he mock him, the man all in green:　　2295
"So now you have your nerve again, I needs must strike;
Uphold the high knighthood that Arthur bestowed,
And keep your neck-bone clear, if this cut allows!"
Then was Gawain gripped with rage, and grimly he said,
"Why, thrash away, tyrant, I tire of your threats;　　　2300
You make such a scene, you must frighten yourself.
Said the green fellow, "In faith, so fiercely you speak
That I shall finish this affair, nor further grace
　　　　　　　　　allow."
　　　　　　　He stands prepared to strike　　　　　2305
　　　　　　　And scowls with both lip and brow;
　　　　　　　No marvel if the man mislike
　　　　　　　Who can hope no rescue now.

He gathered up the grim ax and guided it well:
Let the barb at the blade's end brush the bare throat;　　2310
He hammered down hard, yet harmed him no whit
Save a scratch on one side, that severed the skin;
The end of the hooked edge entered the flesh,
And a little blood lightly leapt to the earth.
And when the man beheld his own blood bright on the snow,　2315
He sprang a spear's length with feet spread wide,
Seized his high helm, and set it on his head,
Shoved before his shoulders the shield at his back,
Bares his trusty blade, and boldly he speaks—
Not since he was a babe born of his mother　　　　　　　2320
Was he once in this world one-half so blithe—
"Have done with your hacking—harry me no more!
I have borne, as behooved, one blow in this place;

If you make another move I shall meet it midway
And promptly, I promise you, pay back each blow   2325
                with brand.
          One stroke acquits me here;
          So did our covenant stand
          In Arthur's court last year—
          Wherefore, sir, hold your hand!"   2330

He lowers the long ax and leans on it there,
Sets his arms on the head, the haft on the earth,
And beholds the bold knight that bides there afoot,
How he faces him fearless, fierce in full arms,
And plies him with proud words—it pleases him well.   2335
Then once again gaily to Gawain he calls,
And in a loud voice and lusty, delivers these words:
"Bold fellow, on this field your anger forbear!
No man has made demands here in manner uncouth,
Nor done, save as duly determined at court.   2340
I owed you a hit and you have it; be happy therewith!
The rest of my rights here I freely resign.
Had I been a bit busier, a buffet, perhaps,
I could have dealt more directly, and done you some harm.
First I flourished with a feint, in frolicsome mood,   2345
And left your hide unhurt—and here I did well
By the fair terms we fixed on the first night;
And fully and faithfully you followed accord:
Gave over all your gains as a good man should.
A second feint, sir, I assigned for the morning   2350
You kissed my comely wife—each kiss you restored.
For both of these there behooved but two feigned blows
                by right.
          True men pay what they owe;
          No danger then in sight.   2355
          You failed at the third throw,
          So take my tap, sir knight.

"For that is my belt about you, that same braided girdle,
My wife it was that wore it; I know well the tale,
And the count of your kisses and your conduct too,   2360
And the wooing of my wife—it was all my scheme!
She made trial of a man most faultless by far
Of all that ever walked over the wide earth;
As pearls to white peas, more precious and prized,
So is Gawain, in good faith, to other gay knights.   2365
Yet you lacked, sir, a little in loyalty there,

But the cause was not cunning, nor courtship either,
But that you loved your own life; the less, then, to blame."
The other stout knight in a study stood a long while,
So gripped with grim rage that his great heart shook.   2370
All the blood of his body burned in his face
As he shrank back in shame from the man's sharp speech.
The first words that fell from the fair knight's lips:
"Accursed be a cowardly and covetous heart!
In you is villainy and vice, and virtue laid low!"   2375
Then he grasps the green girdle and lets go the knot,
Hands it over in haste, and hotly he says:
"Behold there my falsehood, ill hap betide it!
Your cut taught me cowardice, care for my life,
And coveting came after, contrary both   2380
To largesse and loyalty belonging to knights.
Now am I faulty and false, that fearful was ever
Of disloyalty and lies, bad luck to them both!
                    and greed.
          I confess, knight, in this place,   2385
          Most dire is my misdeed;
          Let me gain back your good grace,
          And hereafter I shall take heed."

Then the other laughed aloud, and lightly he said,
"Such harm as I have had, I hold it quite healed.   2390
You are so fully confessed, your failings made known,
And bear the plain penance of the point of my blade,
I hold you polished as a pearl, as pure and as bright
As you had lived free of fault since first you were born.
And I give you, sir, this girdle that is gold-hemmed   2395
And green as my garments, that, Gawain, you may
Be mindful of this meeting when you mingle in throng
With nobles of renown—and known by this token
How it chanced at the Green Chapel, to chivalrous knights.
And you shall in this New Year come yet again   2400
And we shall finish out our feast in my fair hall,
                    with cheer."
          He urged the knight to stay,
          And said, "With my wife so dear
          We shall see you friends this day,   2405
          Whose enmity touched you near."

"Indeed," said the doughty knight, and doffed his high helm,
And held it in his hands as he offered his thanks,
"I have lingered long enough—may good luck be yours,

And He reward you well that all worship bestows!   2410
And commend me to that comely one, your courteous wife,
Both herself and that other, my honoured ladies,
That have trapped their true knight in their trammels so quaint.
But if a dullard should dote, deem it no wonder,
And through the wiles of a woman be wooed into sorrow,   2415
For so was Adam by one, when the world began,
And Solomon by many more, and Samson the mighty—
Delilah was his doom, and David thereafter
Was beguiled by Bathsheba, and bore much distress;
Now these were vexed by their devices—'twere a very joy   2420
Could one but learn to love, and believe them not.
For these were proud princes, most prosperous of old,
Past all lovers lucky, that languished under heaven,
                          bemused.
              And one and all fell prey   2425
              To women that they had used;
              If I be led astray,
              Methinks I may be excused.

"But your girdle, God love you! I gladly shall take
And be pleased to possess, not for the pure gold,   2430
Nor the bright belt itself, nor the beauteous pendants,
Nor for wealth, nor worldly state, nor workmanship fine,
But a sign of excess it shall seem oftentimes
When I ride in renown, and remember with shame
The faults and the frailty of the flesh perverse,   2435
How its tenderness entices the foul taint of sin;
And so when praise and high prowess have pleased my heart,
A look at this love-lace will lower my pride.
But one thing would I learn, if you were not loath,
Since you are lord of yonder land where I have long sojourned   2440
With honor in your house—may you have His reward
That upholds all the heavens, highest on throne!
How runs your right name?—and let the rest go."
"That shall I give you gladly," said the Green Knight then;
"Bertilak de Hautdesert, this barony I hold.[22]   2445
Through the might of Morgan le Fay, that lodges at my house,[23]
By subtleties of science and sorcerers' arts,
The mistress of Merlin, she has caught many a man,
For sweet love in secret she shared sometime
With that wizard, that knows well each one of your knights   2450
                          and you.
              Morgan the Goddess, she,
              So styled by title true;

<blockquote>
None holds so high degree
That her arts cannot subdue.   2455
</blockquote>

"She guided me in this guise to your glorious hall,
To assay, if such it were, the surfeit of pride
That is rumored of the retinue of the Round Table.
She put this shape upon me to puzzle your wits,
To afflict the fair queen, and frighten her to death   2460
With awe of that elvish man that cerily spoke
With his head in his hand before the high table.[24]
She was with my wife at home, that old withered lady,
Your own aunt is she, Arthur's half-sister,
The Duchess' daughter of Tintagel, that dear King Uther   2465
Got Arthur on after, that honored is now.
And therefore, good friend, come feast with your aunt;
Make merry in my house; my men hold you dear,
And I wish you as well, sir, with all my heart,
As any mortal man, for your matchless faith."   2470
But the knight said him nay, that he might by no means.
They clasped then and kissed, and commended each other
To the Prince of Paradise, and parted with one
<blockquote>assent.</blockquote>
<blockquote>
Gawain sets out anew;   2475
Toward the court his course is bent;
And the knight all green in hue,
Wheresoever he wished, he went.
</blockquote>

Wild ways in the world our worthy knight rides
On Gringolet, that by grace had been granted his life.   2480
He harbored often in houses, and often abroad,
And with many valiant adventures verily he met
That I shall not take time to tell in this story.
The hurt was whole that he had had in his neck,
And the bright green belt on his body he bore,   2485
Oblique, like a baldric, bound at his side,
Below his left shoulder, laced in a knot,
In betokening of the blame he had borne for his fault;
And so to court in due course he comes safe and sound.
Bliss abounded in hall when the high-born heard   2490
That good Gawain was come; glad tidings they thought it.
The king kisses the knight, and the queen as well,
And many a comrade came to clasp him in arms,
And eagerly they asked, and awesomely he told,
Confessed all his cares and discomfitures many,   2495
How it chanced at the Chapel, what cheer made the knight,

The love of the lady, the green lace at last.
The nick on his neck he naked displayed
That he got in his disgrace at the Green Knight's hands,
                    alone.   2500
        With rage in heart he speaks,
        And grieves with many a groan;
        The blood burns in his cheeks
        For shame at what must be shown.

"Behold, sir," said he, and handles the belt,   2505
"This is the blazon of the blemish that I bear on my neck;
This is the sign of sore loss that I have suffered there
For the cowardice and coveting that I came to there;
This is the badge of false faith that I was found in there,
And I must bear it on my body till I breathe my last.   2510
For one may keep a deed dark, but undo it no whit,
For where a fault is made fast, it is fixed evermore."
The king comforts the knight, and the court all together
Agree with gay laughter and gracious intent
That the lords and the ladies belonging to the Table,   2515
Each brother of that band, a baldric should have,
A belt borne oblique, of a bright green,
To be worn with one accord for that worthy's sake.
So that was taken as a token by the Table Round,
And he honored that had it, evermore after,   2520
As the best book of knighthood bids it be known.
In the old days of Arthur this happening befell;
The books of Brutus' deeds bear witness thereto
Since Brutus, the bold knight, embarked for this land
After the siege ceased at Troy and the city fared   2525
                    amiss.
        Many such, ere we were born,
        Have befallen here, ere this.
        May He that was crowned with thorn
        Bring all men to His bliss! Amen.   2530

HONI SOIT QUI MAL PENCE[25]

Notes: *Sir Gawain and the Green Knight*

1. line 1: **Since the siege . . . ceased at Troy.** The poet begins his story, as he later ends it, by placing the reign of King Arthur in a broad historical perspective, which includes the fall of Troy. In accordance with medieval notions of history (though not all of his details can be found in the early chronicles), he visualizes Aeneas, son of the king of Troy, and his descendants, as founding a series of western kingdoms to which each gives his name. This westward movement ends with the crossing of the "French Sea" or English Channel, by Brutus, great-grandson of Aeneas, legendary founder of the kingdom of Britain. This Brutus, whom the poet calls *felix* or fortunate, is not to be confused with the Marcus Brutus of Roman history. The deceitful knight of lines 3–4 is evidently Antenor, who in Virgil's *Aeneid* is a trusted counselor, but who appears as a traitor in later versions of the Troy story.

2. lines 109–15: **There Gawain the good knight by Guenevere sits . . . many stalwart knights.** What we are asked to visualize here is not the "Table Round" at which no place was higher or lower than any other, though that table is referred to later by the Green Knight (313). Rather, the poet describes the kind of seating arrangement that he might have seen in a baronial hall, and indeed is still seen in the dining halls at the Universities of Oxford and Cambridge. The "high table," reserved for the most honored guests, stands on a dais opposite the entrance through which the Green Knight will ride. Those seated there face the rest of the company, who occupy tables ranged along either side of the hall (115). The middle seat is the king's, though when the story opens it is vacant. A distinguished representative of the church, Bishop Baldwin, occupies the place of honor at the king's right. Next to the bishop sits Sir Yvain, who, as his partner at table, will share with him the twelve dishes served at the feast (128). At the king's left sits the queen; beside her, Sir Gawain, and beside him, his table partner Sir Agravain.

3. line 182: **A beard big as a bush on his breast hangs.** This detail is one sign of a "generation gap" evidently envisaged by the poet between the Green Knight and the company at King Arthur's court. Abundance of beard and hair bespeak a man past his first youth, as do "bristling eyebrows" such as the Green Knight is said to possess (305). Our attention is again drawn to the beard in line 306, when the knight wags it as he looks around, and in line 334, when he strokes it while awaiting a blow from the ax in the king's hands. His belittling reference to Arthur's knights as "beardless children" (280) further signifies this distance in age between them. Cf. also line 2228.

4. line 186: **Of a king's cap-à-dos:** The word *capados* occurs in this form in Middle English only in *Gawain*, here and in line 572. I have interpreted it, as the poet apparently did also, as *cap-à-dos*—i.e., a garment covering its wearer "from head to back," on the model of *cap-à-pie*, "from head to foot," referring to armor.

5. lines 224–25: **"Where is," he said, "The captain of this crowd?"** The Green Knight's inability, or feigned inability, to tell which of the people before him is King Arthur has insulting implications; in heroic legend, a leader typically stands out in a crowd. In *Beowulf*, for example, the coast guard, greeting the band of Geats on their arrival in the land of the Danes, clearly refers to the hero when

he says "I have never seen a mightier warrior on earth than is one of you. That is no retainer made to seem good by his weapons" (trans. Donaldson).

6. lines 233–34: **For much did they marvel what it might mean / That a horseman and a horse should have such a hue.** The greenness of the Green Knight is susceptible of many interpretations, none of which need preclude the others. It is, most obviously, the color of vegetation, and thus symbolizes the endless vegetative cycle of death and rebirth; the spectators are amazed that a horse and his rider should "grow green as the grass" (235). But this image from the natural realm is immediately discarded in favor of one drawn from the realm of artifice, that of green enamel on gold. And in fact neither can compare, the poet thinks, with the "glorious" hue of the knight. Green also had associations in medieval thought with the infernal realm: a devil in Chaucer's *Friar's Tale,* for example, is dressed all in green. For the members of Arthur's court, the stranger's hue simply enhances his phantasmal and uncanny appearance (239–40).

7. line 477: **"Now, sir, hang up your ax, that has hewn enough."** The "gay" remark with which the king counters the tension of the moment is a witty play on words; the phrase "To hang up one's ax" meant, in Middle English, to stop whatever one has been doing.

8. lines 619–20: **Then they showed forth his shield, that shone all red, / With the pentangle portrayed in purest gold.** The pentangle was a five-pointed star drawn in a continuous line and rejoining itself without a break. In the completed design, the line weaves in and out, going alternately over and under itself. The ancient concept of the five-pointed star merged in medieval thought with that of the six-pointed star of Solomon. Both emblems had magical and religious associations.

9. lines 629–30: **. . . and hence it is called / In all England, as I hear, the endless knot.** But in fact there is no recorded instance of such a phrase.

10. lines 652–54: **. . . beneficence boundless and brotherly love / And pure mind and manners, that none might impeach, / And compassion most precious.** In the poet's Middle English, the names of the five virtues are *franchise, fellowship, cleanness, courtesy,* and *pity.*

11. lines 691–701: **Now he rides in his array through the realm of Logres . . . The Wilderness of Wirral.** The poet evidently thought that Logres, King Arthur's kingdom, was in central or south Wales. Sir Gawain rides north and then turns eastward along the north coast of Wales, leaving Anglesey and its neighboring islands to his left. It was considered dangerous in the poet's time to pass through the forest of Wirral, which was a place of refuge for outlaws and other criminals.

12. line 845: **Broad, bright was his beard, of a beaver's hue.** See note to line 182.

13. lines 897–98: **Tonight you fast and pray; / Tomorrow we'll see you fed.** Those who serve Sir Gawain his meal are joking. On Christmas Eve, as on Fridays and during Lent, Christians were supposed to abstain from meat. The elaborate fish dishes, of course, make the meal anything but an occasion for self-denial.

14. line 950: **But unlike to look upon, those ladies were.** Underlying the double description is a message of religious import: mortal beauty is transitory. Such as the old lady now is, the desirable young lady will be.

15. line 1022: **The joys of St. John's Day were justly praised.** The date of St. John's Day is December 27, so there are four days left, not three, before the New Year's morning on which Sir Gawain is bound to set out to meet the Green Knight. But he lies late in bed at the lord's behest only three days. A line after 1022 may inadvertently have been omitted; in any case, a day seems to be missing.

16. line 1141: **Blew upon their bugles bold blasts three.** Three long notes, or *motes*, were sounded when the hunters unleashed the hounds. The words used by the poet are *thre bare mote*, an onomatopoeic sequence of three long syllables, which I have replicated in my version of the line.

17. lines 1239–40: **Your servant to command / I am, and shall be still.** *Servant* could have its innocuous modern meaning ("one who would be glad to be of service") in the poet's Middle English. But it also meant specifically "a professed lover." Sir Gawain takes advantage of this ambiguity in line 1278.

18. line 1325: **The lords lent a hand.** The skills proper to a nobleman in the poet's time included the dressing—disemboweling and dismembering—of deer killed in the hunt.

19. line 1347: **And this they named the numbles.** The modern expression "humble pie" comes from *umble*, a variant form of *numble*.

20. line 1355: **The corbie's bone they cast on a branch.** *Corbie* is a name for the raven (cf. French *corbeau*). Ravens, being carrion birds, would in all probability stay close at hand during the butchering that followed a hunt. It was customary to throw a small piece of gristle into the branches of a nearby tree for them.

21. lines 1880–81: **And shamefaced at shrift he showed his misdeeds / From the largest to the least, and asked the Lord's mercy.** Gawain evidently does not confess his intention of withholding from the lord the girdle he has been given by the lady, thus failing to live up to the terms of their agreement. Because the intention to commit a sin (in this case primarily the sin of failing to be true to one's word) is itself sinful, his confession would seem to be invalid. Perhaps, as has been suggested, he feels that it is not sinful to break the rules of a mere "game" (1111). But he feels differently later, as is shown by his outburst in lines 2378–84. However Gawain's confession and absolution at Hautdesert are to be interpreted, it is fair to say that the absolution that strikes most readers of the poem as "real" is the secular one Sir Gawain receives later from the Green Knight (2391–94).

22. line 2445: **"Bertilak de Hautdesert, this barony I hold."** The first name appears, though it is of minor importance, in Arthurian tradition. A Bertolais and a Bertelak figure in two stories, one French and one English, but neither one has the slightest resemblance to the Green Knight. The name *Hautdesert* is not found elsewhere; it seems to be composed of two French words that would mean "high hermitage," and would thus imply the isolation of Lord Bertilak's castle from other human dwellings.

23. line 2446. **Through the might of Morgan le Fay, that lodges at my house.** Morgan le Fay, a famous "fairy" or enchantress, was, as we hear later (2464), the half-sister of King Arthur. (Why she should be a member of Lord Bertilak's household is not so clear.) Merlin, her lover, was a magician who plays an important role in a number of the Arthurian stories. See the note to lines 2456–62.

24. lines 2456–62: **"She guided me in this guise to your glorious hall. . . . /**

before the high table." Few readers of the poem have been satisfied by this explanation of the opening episode. It is, however, in keeping with a tradition to the effect that Morgan le Fay was a bitter enemy of Queen Guenevere.

25. **HONI SOIT QUI MAL PENCE,** or "Evil be to him who evil thinks," is the motto of the Order of the Garter. The words have been added to the manuscript, apparently by someone who thought there was, or wanted to suggest, a relationship between the adoption of the green girdle by Arthur's court and the founding of the Order in 1350. But there is general agreement that there is little basis for interpreting one in terms of the other (for one thing, the ceremonial Garter is not green but blue). By allowing the motto to stand after the concluding "Amen," as it does in the manuscript, I do not mean to indicate that I consider it part of the poem.

Patience

Introduction

Story and Style

For most readers, insofar as they know it at all, the story told in the biblical Book of Jonah is remote from reality. It unfolds not only in a far-off time and place but on a plane higher than that on which we live our everyday lives. Its major character is a prophet who converses regularly with the one God of the Old Testament; and its major event, the swallowing of the prophet by a whale followed by his three-day sojourn in its belly, is not only miraculous but impossible to imagine as happening to us or anyone like us. Reading the story in the Old Testament, we find it told in spare, terse language, ungarnished by descriptive detail or commentary. The first chapter begins:

> 1 Now the word of the Lord came to Jonas the son of Amathi, saying:
> 2 Arise, and go to Ninive the great city, and preach in it: for the wickedness thereof is come up before me.
> 3 And Jonas rose up to flee into Tharsis from the face of the Lord.

(The Book of Jonah in its entirety is printed in "Biblical Sources," p. 105.) Not until the fourth and final chapter of the book do we hear, from Jonah himself, an explanation for—or at least a rationalization of—his refusal to obey God's command. In biblical translations such as the one I have quoted, the story is further distanced from us by its language. Words like *arise* and *thereof* and idioms like *is come* have for a long time been largely restricted to religious and ceremonial contexts; they have taken on a corresponding elevation and solemnity of tone.

An important part of what the poet does in retelling the Book of Jonah is to turn its story into a human comedy, though the poem also includes a number of serious passages that enlarge its meaning, as I shall explain later. Its central figure, we soon see, is someone who, though he is a divinely ordained prophet, is very much like our fallible selves, someone who responds with reluctance, much as we would, to the peremptory and disagreeable commands of his lord. (In this, he is typical of the Old Testament prophets generally.) His sea journey, the storm that nearly wrecks his ship, his descent into the belly of the whale, his three days' sojourn there, and his adventures in and around Niniveh—all are dramatized with brilliant realism. As when we look at a stereoscopic image, we are drawn irresistibly into simulated three-dimensional space. Observing Jonah's actions and reactions, even if we are aware that we are in a sense reading the Bible, we are more apt to shake our heads and smile than to nod solemnly.

The Moral Message

But the author of *Patience* is not entertaining us with comedy for comedy's sake; he is intent on driving home an overt moral message. For him, the biblical story of Jonah illustrated the importance in human life of what he thought of as "patience": *patience* is the first word in the poem, and its first line singles patience out as a "point," or topic, or aspect of behavior, worth talking about. (In my translation, I take advantage of the proverb "Patience is a virtue.") But the concept of patience, in the poet's time, was larger and more important than it is in ours. We think of a patient person as one who, in an unpleasant or tedious situation—say, standing in a long line—waits uncomplainingly for it to come to an end. Conceived of in this way, it is a relatively trivial and, as it were, occasional, virtue. But in the medieval period, especially in religious thought, the meaning of the word reflected fully its Latin origin in the present participle, *patiens*, of the verb *patior*, "to bear or endure" (from the past participle of the same verb comes the word *passive*). To be patient was to be submissive in the very general sense of accepting one's situation in life, especially when it was unfortunate, as decreed by God. *Patience* and *suffering* thus were akin in meaning, and indeed "to suffer," in Middle English, meant not only "to endure pain" but "to wait patiently." (Our adjective *long-suffering* reflects this earlier sense.)

Inevitably, patience in medieval thought was associated in particular with low social status and thus with poverty, and the poor were regularly exhorted to aspire to it. One of the proverbs in the *Dicta* or sayings of Dionysius Cato, a collection popular in medieval times and often cited by Chaucer, advocates patient endurance of the burden of poverty. The connection between the two goes back to the life of Jesus: he himself had been "patient" in submitting himself to mortality, and finally to suffering and death on the cross, to redeem humankind. He had remained poor by choice and had imposed poverty on his disciples as part of their way of life. And he had advocated patience as a response to aggression, saying that whoever was struck on one cheek should turn his head and offer the other. Patience continued to be of central importance among Christian virtues in early times, when the church was suffering persecution at the hands of those in power. In the Gospel of Luke, Jesus predicted that his followers would be imprisoned, and some of them put to death, for his sake, and he told them, "In patience you shall possess your souls." St. Paul in his letters spoke of his own patience in enduring the punishments imposed on him during his travels as a missionary and exhorted his followers to follow his example.

Use of Biblical Sources

The poet who wrote *Patience* knew his Bible thoroughly. Like other scholars of his time, he thought of it as one great whole whose every part literally or symbolically signified some aspect of Christian history or doctrine. A ready way of interpreting a given passage was to bring other passages to bear on it; anything in the Old Testament, in particular, could be seen as prefiguring something in the New. Identifying his theme in the Book of Jonah, the *Patience*-poet found it also in the famous series of eight virtues, each bringing its possessor a blessing or reward, known as the Beatitudes. These appear in a sermon by Jesus recorded in chapter 5 of the Gospel of Matthew; there is a much shorter version in Luke 6. (The passages from Matthew and Luke are printed in "Biblical Sources," p. 105.) The first and the eighth Beatitude in Matthew read, "Blessed are the poor in spirit" and "Blessed are they that suffer persecution for justice' sake," and exactly the same reward is predicted in both, namely, "For theirs is the kingdom of heaven." In the Vulgate Bible that was known to the *Patience*-poet, the eighth Beatitude reads "Beati qui persecutionem patiuntur" (Blessed who suffer persecution), *patiuntur* being a form of the same Latin verb that I identified earlier as the source of the word *patience*. In interpreting the first Beatitude, the poet disregards the qualification of "poor" by "in spirit" and interprets *poor* as having its primary, material meaning (he has a precedent in the Gospel of Luke, where the corresponding verse reads simply "Blessed are ye poor"). He thus can see the two as linked not only by the fact that they promise the same reward but by the traditional connection between poverty and patience.

In the opening section of the poem (1–60), the speaker, after praising patience, paraphrases the series of eight Beatitudes and goes on to personify them playfully as eight "dames," calling the first one "Dame Poverty" and the last one "Dame Patience." He himself, he says, is fated to live in poverty, so it behooves him to acquire patience also, for where poverty is present, men must summon up patience to endure it. He goes on to speak of the futility of resisting the hardships a poor man must endure, particularly as a servitor who, whether he likes it or not, must do the bidding of his lord. Even if he were told to ride as far as Rome, there would be no use grumbling. Complaints are futile; in the end, he will have to carry out the original order, and he will have made his lord angry at him. This reminds him of how God commanded Jonah to undertake a long journey, how Jonah tried to evade the command, and what happened to him as a result. For the first time, the speaker explicitly addresses an audience that presumably has been listening to him all along; if they will pay attention to him for a little while, he will tell them the story as it is told in the Bible.

The putting together of the Old and New Testaments had begun in the New Testament itself. Jesus alluded to the Book of Jonah when he prophesied, "For as Jona[h] was in the whale's belly three days and three nights: so shall the Son of man be in the heart of the earth three days and three nights" (Matthew 12.40). The swallowing of Jonah by the whale and his emergence from its belly unharmed were thus considered to be "types" of the death and resurrection of Jesus—that is, they were interpreted as real events that anticipated later ones. Such correspondences were part of the design of "salvation history": the fall of humankind as recounted in Genesis, the history of Israel, the compensatory incarnation of God's son as the man Jesus, his suffering and death, his resurrection, and the resultant redemption of those who believed in him as the Messiah. The whale in the Book of Jonah was further identified by medieval scholars with the sea monster referred to as "leviathan" in the Book of Job, in the rhetorical question asked of Job by God: "Canst thou draw out the leviathan with a hook?" Because the whale's action in swallowing Jonah prefigured the death of Jesus, the whale was thought of as a type of Satan, the bringer of death into the world, who seized figuratively upon Jesus's mortal flesh when he died on the Cross but had to release it when death was defeated by the resurrection. On the medieval stage, the monster whose enormous gaping mouth represented the entrance to hell was sometimes portrayed as a whale.

We could have assumed that the *Patience*-poet was aware of these interpretive connections. But in fact we know he was, because he makes use of them in telling his story. The obstinately rebellious behavior of Jonah in refusing to go to Niniveh to preach is the exact opposite of the behavior of Jesus—Jonah is not so much a type of Jesus as an antitype—and the poet sharpens this antithesis by reminding us of Jesus as he recounts Jonah's actions. When he says, for example, that Jonah set out for Tarshish because he was unwilling to suffer any of the torments that were likely to befall him at the hands of the Ninivites, he uses, to signify "torments," the word *pines*. *Pine* as a noun has died out by now; as a verb, it is restricted to a few expressions such as "to pine away." In Middle English, however, the noun was in common use. It primarily meant "suffering"; it had strong religious associations; and it specifically designated the sufferings of Jesus on the Cross. (Chaucer has one of his pilgrims in *The Canterbury Tales* swear "by God's sweet pine.") And the torments themselves, as Jonah anxiously imagines them, conspicuously include crucifixion: God will care little, he thinks, if he is stripped naked and torn apart on a cross.

As for the whale, his Satanic character is indicated at several points in the narrative. The poet calls him a *warlowe* or demon in line 258 (I translate "hell-monster") and says that the inside of his belly "stank like the devil" and "reeked of hell" (274–75). When Jonah prays to God from the whale's interior, he says that God has heard him out of "Hell's dark womb" (306). He also complains that his body is imprisoned in the "abyss" (318). The Middle English form of this word meant both "the depths of the sea" and "the bottomless pit," i.e., "hell."

Variation of Tone

These references to Satan and to damnation, like the references to "the kingdom of heaven" in the paraphrased Beatitudes, serve to remind the members of the poem's audience that they live in a world in which sin is punished and goodness rewarded in the afterlife, according to the judgment of the Christian God. But the outlook of the poem as it begins is pragmatic, and its morality is firmly grounded in this world. The rewards of patience described in the opening section (and in part in the poem's conclusion) are to be expected in this life rather than in the next. We should avoid impatience primarily because it aggravates our earthly troubles rather than relieving them; if we tear our clothes in exasperation, we will just have to sew them up later (527–28).

Even God, who in the final episode emerges as the most important character in the story, is portrayed as understandable in human terms. It is true that he is the Sovereign sitting on his celestial throne (93–94) who created the world out of nothing and has absolute power over it; Jonah identifies him to his shipmates as "the one God whose will all obey," who "wrought with his word" the heavens, the earth, and all living things. God himself points out in his speech at the end of the poem that he created not only the inhabitants of Niniveh (including among these, presumably, the "dumb beasts" that eat the grasses and the broom plants) but the primordial "matter" out of which, in turn, they were shaped. But if he is the Lord all-powerful, he is equally the Father all-merciful—"oure mercyable God," as the poet calls him. The king of Niniveh, who knows him by reputation, is aware that graciousness is an aspect of his nobility; he may well decide to spare him and his people when they have repented. And Jonah's angry justification of his original refusal to go to Niniveh stems partly from his knowledge of this aspect of God's nature: "I knew well your courteous ways, your wise forbearance, / . . . / Your leniency, your longsuffering, your delayed vengeance; / And ever mercy in full measure, though the misdeed be huge" (417–20).

Even God's omnipotence, however, seems to differ from human power in degree rather than in kind. The passage the poet quotes from Psalm 93 (numbered 94 in the A.V.), to the effect that the creator of human sight and hearing must have those faculties himself, implies that God is the same sort of being that we are. He is also made "human" in being, or at least seeming, fallible. When he first speaks to Jonah of his vexation with the Ninivites, his manner strongly suggests the impatience we have just heard criticized. He addresses Jonah "roughly and rudely," without any provocation that we know of. Nor is he long-suffering. On the contrary, he says he is so angry that he can't wait to be avenged; Jonah must drop whatever he is doing and go to Niniveh immediately. What is more, both the Bible and the medieval poet state flatly that in sparing the city, God is going back on his word. And his inconsistency makes a liar out of his prophet. Jonah's words to God in the biblical story leave this charge implicit, but the Middle English Jonah comes right out with it (428).

Jonah, then, has some cause to be aggrieved. But the poet makes him seem so petulant, so childishly self-centered in his complaints about both the sparing of Niniveh and the destruction of his sheltering woodbine, that amusement qualifies our sympathy. It is God's point of view that prevails: after he has explained why he acted as he did, we hear nothing more from Jonah. And this is as it should be: what, after all, is one prophet's reputation for accuracy as against the destruction of a great city filled not only with repentant sinners but with many who never sinned at all?

The moral the poem began with, that patience is the best remedy for the pains life inflicts on us, is thus finally supplemented by another, that God, because he loves the human beings he created, is patient with them, ready to pardon them if, having done evil, they repent. As we look back from Jonah's angry outbursts toward the end of the story to his earlier words, we find God's infinite mercy, along with his infinite power, praised in passages that are not part of the comedy, passages that add to it a strain of poignant eloquence. Such a passage is Jonah's profession of faith on shipboard:

> I worship the one God whose will all obey:
> The wide world with the welkin, the wind and the stars,
> And all that range in that realm, he wrought with his word. (206–8)

Such, too, is his prayer from the whale's belly, which in the Bible, as in the poet's Middle English, is reminiscent of the mixture of complaint, prayer, and reverent praise characteristic of the Psalms (I have footnoted some specific echoes in the text below). These passages must be taken seriously. The mixture of the ludicrous and the sacred, familiarity and reverence, presented by the poem is typical of an age in which religious imagery was part of the fabric of everyday life. It may remind us of the realistic drawings and caricatures in a medieval psalter, on a page where we also see a picture of the Virgin holding her child.

The Ending

Some scholars, reading the poem in the original, have been perplexed by a problem of wording posed by its first line. As is also true in *Pearl* and *Sir Gawain and the Green Knight*, the end of the poem echoes its beginning. But in *Patience* there is a conspicuous difference between the two. The first line, as I said earlier, calls patience "a point," but the last line calls it "a noble point." Did the poet mean to include the adjective at the beginning as well, and did the copyist then omit it by mistake? I am among those who think not: the heightened praise of patience at the conclusion reflects an enlargement of thought that has taken place in the course of the narrative. Patience is now associated not just with "pain" but with "penance" (531). This additional concept, of course, comes out of the story of the Ninivites, who wore hair shirts and fasted, lamenting their sins. And it bears directly on the lives of the medieval Christians who made up the audience of the poem, guided as they were by the authority of the church. God's patience with the repentant Ninivites shows that the sorrow of sinners over having sinned and their willing endurance of the assigned pains of penance will assuredly bring not only God's forgiveness, but the ultimate happiness promised in the Beatitudes to those who are patient: theirs will be the kingdom of heaven. Conceived of thus, patience is more than just a virtue helping us to bear our troubles from day to day. It is a great virtue indeed, operating on a scale transcending the human life span as part of the perfection of God himself.

A Note on the Embarcation (Lines 101–8)

The poet's description of the departure from Joppa of the ship Jonah had boarded there is of interest because it illustrates not only his habitual expansion and elaboration of his biblical source but his interest in and knowledge of technical skills and the terms pertaining to them, as is also shown in the hunting scenes in *Sir Gawain and the Green Knight*. Both the description and the account of the voyage strongly suggest that he had at some time before he wrote the poem experienced an actual voyage at sea.

He refers to the ship specifically as a *cog*. The cog, a large sailing ship, came into use in the thirteenth and fourteen centuries. It had a single mast amidships and a single square sail, called in the language of the original poem a *crossayl* (102) (see figure, page 88). This was hoisted aloft while still furled on its spar, and let down by guy ropes or guide ropes when the ship was about to get under way (105). Such a ship could sail only directly, or somewhat obliquely, before the wind; in the latter case, a sheet called the *bowline* was led forward from the windward side of the sail to the bowsprit

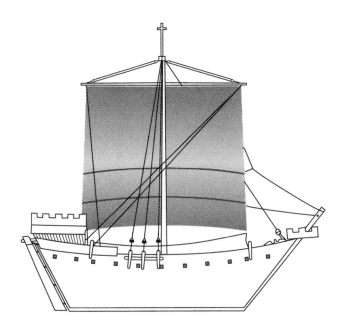

A Medieval Cog.

(104) so that the sail would not swing round and spill the wind. The poet's account indicates that the ship was anchored at the dock with the wind blowing across it. After letting down the sail, the sailors pushed off with oars on the port or larboard side of the bow (106); this is evidently what is meant by the wording of the original, "they laid in to larboard." Oars are resorted to later, during the storm (217). (The poet's word, *ladde-borde*, in line 106 is an earlier form of *larboard*, which originally meant "loading side." *Larboard* was later changed to *port*, i.e., "port" or "dock" side, apparently to avoid confusion with the similar word *starboard*.) The sail "luffed," or flapped (106), until the wind was astern of it, at which point its "bosom" or belly (107) filled and the ship began to move forward (108) (see figure, page 89).

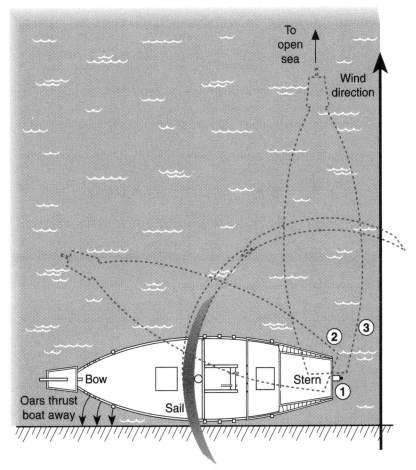

Port, or larboard, side

How Jonah's Ship Was Propelled Out of the Harbor

Patience†

Patience is a virtue, though vexing it prove.
When heavy hearts are hurt by hateful deeds
Longsuffering may assuage them and soothe the smart,
For she mends all things marred, and mitigates malice.
Who possessed his soul in patience would prosper in time;   5
Who balks at his burdens is beset the more;
Then better for me to bear the brunt as it befalls
Than harp on my hardships, though my heart mislike.
I heard on a holy day, at a high mass,
How the Master taught the multitude, as Matthew tells,   10
Eight blessings in order,[1] each with a reward,
Set singularly, in sequence, as suited each one.*
They are happy, he said, who in heart are poor,
For theirs is heaven's kingdom to hold for ever;
They are happy who have the habit of meekness,   15
For they shall reign as they will in every realm of this world;
They are happy likewise who weep for their harms,
For comfort in many countries shall come to their souls;
They are happy also who hunger after right,
For they shall freely be refreshed and filled with all good;   20
They are happy also who in heart have pity,
For mercy shall be meted them in measure unstinting;
They are happy also who in heart are pure,
For they shall see the best of sights: the Savior enthroned;
They are happy also who hold their peace,[2]   25
For the sons of God's self they shall solemnly be called;
They are happy who guide well and govern their hearts,[3]
For theirs is heaven's kingdom, as you heard before.
These blessings were preached us in promise of bliss
If we would love these ladies and liken us to them: 30
Dame Poverty, Dame Pity, Dame Penance the third,
Dame Meekness, Dame Mercy, Dame Purity most pleasant,

† Notes for *Patience* appear on pages 103–4.
* Matthew 5.3–10.

And then Dame Peace and Dame Patience put in thereafter;
He were happy who had one; to have all were better.
But since a plight called Poverty is appointed me here,   35
I shall pair her with Patience and play along with both;
For these two are a team, in the text as they stand;
They are fashioned in one form, the first and the last,
And the wages of their wise ways are one and the same;
And also, as I see it, they are the same in kind: 40
Where Poverty is in place, no power can dislodge her,
For she lingers on at her leisure, like it or not,
And where Poverty oppresses and pinches a man,
Let him prate never so loud, perforce he must bear it.
Thus Poverty and Patience are playfellows, I find;   45
Since I am beset by them both, it behooves me to suffer.
Then let me rather like them and laud their ways
Than frown and be froward and fare all the worse.
If a destiny is dealt me and duly comes round,
What avail my vexation and venting of spleen?   50
Or if the lord of my land, whose liege man I am,
Bids me ride or else run to Rome on his errand,
What gain I by grumbling but greater grief still?
He would make good his mastery, or I much mistake,
And threaten me, and think me an unthankful knave,   55
When the terms of my tenure should have taught me to bow.
Did not Jonah in Judea a bold jaunt begin?
In search of his own safety, he serves himself ill.
If you will tarry a little time, and attend to my story,
You shall have the whole truth, as Holy Writ tells.   60
It is entered of old in the annals of Judea:
Prophet there to the Gentiles was Jonah professed.
He got words from God that gave him no joy:
A rough summons and rude resounds in his ears:
"Rise, rest no longer, make ready to travel;   65
Fare forth to Niniveh without further speech;
Sow my words in the ways of that wide city,
As at that place, at that point, I put in your heart.
For all are so evil that harbor therein,
And their malice is so monstrous, I can no more withhold   70
My vengeance from their vile deeds, with venom ingrained.
Speed now to Niniveh and speak as I bid."
When the stern voice fell still, that astounded him sore,
His mind was moved to anger—he muttered to himself,
"If I obey His bidding and bring them this tale,   75
And am taken and detained there, my troubles begin.

He says those sinners are consummate knaves;
I come with those tidings, they accost me straightway,
Pen me in a prison, put me in stocks,
Gall my feet with fetters, gouge out my eyes.   80
A marvelous message for a man to preach
Among cruel foes countless, and cursèd fiends!
—Unless my dear Lord on my downfall is bent
For the sake of some misdeed deserving of death.
At all costs, I shall take care to keep my distance: 85
I shall go off some other way, out of His ken;
I shall take a trip to Tarshish and tarry there a while,
And if I lie low and am lost, He will leave me in peace."
He rises, rests no longer, makes ready to travel,
Jonah to Port Joppa; joyless, he growls   90
That by no means will he meekly submit so to suffer,
Though his Father value little the life that He formed.
"He sits there," says he, "on His seat so high
In His glory and grandeur—small gloom He feels
If I am seized now in Niniveh and naked displayed,   95
Racked on a rough cross by ruffians ungodly."
So he passes to the port, his passage to seek,
Finds there a fair ship fitted out to sail,
Parleys with the mariners, pays his money
To be taken with no tarrying to Tarshish that day.   100
He goes across by the gangplank; they get their gear ready,
Bend on the big sail, belay their cables,
Set the windlass working, weigh anchors forthwith;
The bowline to the bowsprit briskly they fasten,
Grip well the guy-ropes: the great canvas falls.   105
They lay oars to larboard, she luffs in the breeze
Till the blithe breath at her back finds the bosom of the sail
And sweeps their sweet ship for them swift from the harbor.[4]
Was never so joyous a Jew as Jonah was then,
Who had schemed to escape unscathed from his Lord.   110
He thought the Almighty, who made all the world,
Could do him no damage on the deep sea—
Why, the witless wretch! He who would not obey
Soon finds himself in a fix and faces more danger.
That was a senseless presumption that seized his mind,   115
When he set out from Samaria, that God saw no farther:
Yes, His gaze went wide enough, as he well might have known.
The wise words of the king had warned him often,
Royal David on dais, who endited this speech
In a psalm that he sang and set in the Psalter: 120

"O fools that walk the world, find wisdom for once,
And strive to understand, for all your stark folly:
Think you He has no hearing, whose hand formed the ear?
It cannot be that He is blind who built each bright eye."°
But this dull-witted dotard dreads not God's hand;　　　　　125
He is out on the high seas, heading for Tarshish.
But he was traced in a trice as he traveled, I find,
And the shaft he had shot fell shamefully short,
For the Master whose mind commands all knowledge,
Who wakes ever and watches, His will is well served.　　　　　130
He called on his craftworks, creatures of His hand;
The angrier was their answer, for angrily He called:
"Eurus and Aquilon, east-dwelling winds,⁵
Blow with both your breaths over bleak waters."
There was little time lost once the Lord had spoken:　　　　　135
Straightway they bestir them to strike as He bids.
And now out of the northeast the noise begins
As they blow with both their breaths over bleak waters;
The cloud-rack runs ragged, reddening beneath;
The ocean howls hellishly, awful to hear;　　　　　140
The winds on the wan water so wildly contend
That the surges ascending are swept up so high
And then drawn back to the depths, that fear-dazed fish
Dare not rest, for that rage, at the roiled sea-bottom.
When wind and waves as one had worked their will　　　　　145
All joyless was the jolly boat Jonah had boarded;
For she reeled all around upon the rough waves;
The shock of the after wind shattered all her gear,
Hurled helter-skelter the helm and the stern,
Tore loose her tackle, toppled her mast;　　　　　150
The sail swam on the sea; the deck swaying down
Must drink ever deeper, and now the din rises.
They cut cords from the cargo and cast it away;
Many a lad leapt forth to unloose and to cast;
They bailed the baneful water, bent on escape,　　　　　155
For though we like our lot but little, life is ever sweet.
So they hauled and they hoisted and heaved over the side
Their bags and their featherbeds and their bright-hued clothes,
Their coffers of costly goods, their casks and their chests,
All to lighten their load, if relief could be had.　　　　　160
But the winds, unwearying, blew wilder than ever,
And the maelstrom ever madder and more to be feared,

° Psalm 93.8–9 (A.V. 94).

Till, wearied out and woeful, they worked no more,
But each turned to the god in whose grace he trusted.
Some to Vernagu devoutly vouchsafed their prayers;   165
Some addressed them to Diana and doom-dealing Neptune;
To Mohammed and Magog,[6] the Moon and the Sun,
As each followed his faith and had fixed his heart.
Then up spoke the wisest, well-nigh despairing:
"I believe there is some outlaw, some disloyal wretch,   170
Who has grieved his god and goes here among us;
For his sins we are sinking and soon will perish.
Let us now lay a lottery alike upon all,
And whoso is singled out, send him into the water,
And when the evil one is ousted, what else can we trust   175
But that the ruler of the rain-cloud will let the rest be?"
They assented to this speech, and summoned were all
From every corner of that craft, to come and stand trial.
A steersman stepped lively to search under hatches
For any who were absent, to add to the roll.   180
But of those he thought to find, he was thwarted by one,
And that was Jonah the Jew, abject in hiding.
He has fled for fear of the fury of the storm
Into the bottom of the boat, a board for his bed,
Huddled aft in the hold, hard by the rudder,   185
And there he snoozes and snores and slobbers unsightly.
The man gives him a good kick to make him get up—
May Ragnel in shackles[7] shake him out of his dreams!—
By the clasp of his cloak he clutches him fast,
Drags him up on deck, and down he sits him,   190
And rudely requires of him what reason he has
In such onslaughts of the sea to sleep so sound.
Now they tally their tokens; each takes one in turn,
And from first round to last, the lot falls on Jonah.
Then they glare at him grimly, and gruffly demand,   195
"What the devil have you done, dotard wretch?
What seek you out at sea, sinful knave,
With your damnable deeds that will drown us all?
Have you no governor nor god to give ear to your prayers,
That in danger of death you drop off to sleep?   200
From what country do you come? What crave you abroad?
Whither lies your way, and what is your errand?
See, your doom now descends for your deeds ill-done:
Do homage to your deity ere we dip you under."
"I am a Hebrew," said he, "and Israel-born;   205
I worship the one God whose will all obey:

The wide world with the welkin, the wind and the stars,
And all that range in that realm, He wrought with His word.
All this mischief on my account is made at this time,
For I have grieved my God, and guilty He finds me,   210
So send me over the rail into the rough sea,
Or you get of Him no grace, I give you my word."
He made them understand, by the story that he told,
That he had fled from the face of his far-seeing lord;
Then such a fear befell them, they fainted in heart,   215
And heeded him no longer, but made haste to row.
They laid hands on long oars and lugged them in place,
And set them along the sides, for their sail was lost,
And strained with every stroke, and strove to escape,
But their power was as nothing; it would not prevail.   220
In the black boiling surge their oarblades broke;
Then they had no help in hand in that hapless plight,
Nor was there comfort to cling to, nor course to follow
But deal Jonah the judgment that justice decreed.
First they prayed to the Prince that prophets serve   225
That he let them off lightly, nor unleash his wrath
Though in innocent blood they bathed their hands,
And it was his man and messenger they meant to destroy.
Then by top and by toe they tossed him out,
Handed him over in haste to the hateful water;   230
No sooner had he touched it than the tempest ceased;
The waves made peace with the wind in the wink of an eye.
Though they teetered and tilted, with tackle torn loose,
Strong streaming currents constrained them awhile,
And briskly bore them on, by behest of the deep,   235
Till a sweeter one swept them swift to the shore.
When they reached that place of rest, they reverently prayed
To our merciful God, as Moses taught,
With sacrifice unstinted, and solemn vows,
And said he was the sole God, and forsook all others.   240
Though they are jocund and joyous, Jonah yet fears;
Yes, he finds his fortune fickle, who fled from all harm.
What befell that foolish man from the time he hit water,
It were hard to believe, had Holy Writ not been.
Now is Jonah the Jew in jeopardy dire;   245
From that storm-shaken ship they shove him straightway.
A wild wallowing whale, by some whim of fate,
That had been driven from the depths, drew near that place
And saw a man seized and sent into the sea,
And swiftly swerved and made a swoop, on swallowing bent.   250

The men still holding his toes, the huge mouth takes him;
Untouched by any tooth, he tumbles down his throat.
Then he sounds° and descends to the sea bottom,
Amid ridges of rough rock and racing currents,
And the man in his maw half-demented with dread,   255
As little wonder it was if woe possessed him,
For had the hand of heaven's King, that holds all the world,
Not helped this hapless wretch in hell-monster's guts,
What lore or what law could lead us to think
That any life might be allowed him so long there within?   260
But he was succored by the Sovereign that sits on high,
Though he had no hope of help in the innards of that fish,
And was driven through the deep and dashed about in darkness:
Lord, cold was his comfort and his care huge!
For he remembered each mishap that he had met with that day, 265
How 'twixt the boat and the briny he was borne off by a whale,
And thrown into his throat without threat or warning;
As a mote in at a minster door, so mighty were his jaws.
He glides in by the gills through glistening slime,
Goes down a gut that guides him like a road,   270
Ever head over heels hurtling along,
To a broad block of space as big as a hall,
And there he fixed his feet firmly and stretched forth his arms,
And stood up in his stomach, that stank like the devil;
Thus in rot and corruption that reeked of hell   275
Was his dwelling ordained, who deigned not to suffer!
Then he casts about busily, where best he can find
Some haven in that hulk, but beholds evermore
No place of rest or rescue, but rampant filth,
Whichever gut his eyes gaze on, but God is still sweet,   280
And so he held him steady a space, and spoke to his Lord:
"Now, Prince, have pity on your prophet here;
Though I am foolish and fickle, and false of heart,
Let the power of compassion put vengeance aside.
I am guilty of guile, I am gall and wormwood,   285
But you are God, and all good in your governance lies.
Have mercy now on your man and his misdeeds,
And show yourself true sovereign over sea and land."
With that he crept to a corner and couched him therein,
Where he was free of the filth that defiled the place,   290
And there he sat as safe and sound, save for darkness only,
As in the bottom of the boat where before he had slept.

° *He:* the whale. *Sounds:* sinks himself.

So in a bowel of that beast he bides his time,
Three days and three nights, ever thinking of God,
His might and his mercy, his measured judgments;   295
Now he knows him in dire need, who knew him not in plenty.
And this whale wallows on over watery wastes,
Through many regions wild and rough, so restive he was,
For that mote in his maw, though by measure of bulk
It were nothing next to him, made a niggling in his belly.   300
And as he sailed on and on, incessantly he heard
The big sea on his back and beating on his sides.
Then the prophet composed a prayer to his God;
These were his thoughts, and thus did he speak them:
"I have looked to you, Lord, lamenting my cares;°   305
You heard me when I was hid in Hell's dark womb;†
My feeble voice failed, yet you found me out;
You dipped me into the dim heart of the deep waters;
The great surge of your seas besets me about:
Your freshets overflowing, your unfathomed pools,   310
And your currents in their courses contending together,
All raging in a race, roll over my head.°°
And yet I said, when I was set at the sea-bottom,
Doleful am I, denied the dear light of your eyes,
And dissevered from your sight, yet some day I know   315
I shall tread your temple floor and return to your service.
I am walled around with water through my woe's term;
The abyss binds my body, I bide there in thrall;
The seething of the sea-swirl sounds over my head;
I am borne to the last bourne, the base of the mountains.   320
Each bank is a barrier beating me back
From the landfall I long for; my fate lies with you.
You shall yet save your servant, set justice aside
Through the mildness of your mercy that is most to trust.††
For when the onset of anguish ached in my soul   325
Then I hoped, as behooved, in heaven's great Lord,
That he would pity his prophet, pay heed to my prayer,
That my orisons might enter his most holy house.
I have listened to your learned folk many a long day,
But now I see for certain that those unsound minds   330
That devote them to vanities and vain pursuits,
Forego the grace they are given for gewgaws and trifles.

° Psalm 119.1 (A.V. 120).
† Psalm 129.1–2 (A.V. 130).
°° Psalm 68.2–3 (A.V. 69.1–2).
†† Psalm 68.14–17 (A.V. 69.13–16); Psalm 6.5 (A.V. 6.4).

But I vow most devoutly, and in veriest truth,
That I shall solemnly sacrifice when I am safe at last,
And honor you with an offering whole and entire,   335
And hold to your each behest, have here my word."
Then our Father bids the fish with forceful voice
That he heave him out hastily on land high and dry.
The whale at this word finds his way to a shore,
And there he pukes up the prophet as compelled by our Lord.   340
Then he was swept onto the sand in beslobbered clothes—
It would have been as well to have washed his mantle!
The beach and lands beyond that he beheld there
Were of the very region he had run from before.
Then a wind of God's word whipped past his ears: 345
"So, you'll not go to Niniveh? You know no way thither?"
"Yes, Lord of my life—do but lend me the grace
To go with your good will; else gain I nothing."
"Rise, approach then to preach—lo, the place lies beyond!
My lore is locked within you; unloose it there!"   350
Then he rested no longer, but rose and set forth;
By night he had drawn near to Niniveh's walls.
Now this city was wondrous in width and in length:
To traverse it entirely took a man three days.
A full day's journey had Jonah performed   355
Ere he said a single word to a soul that he met,
And then he cried with such a clamor as caught every ear;
The tenor of his true text he told in this way:
"When forty days fully are finished and past,
Niniveh shall be made nought, as it had never been.   360
I tell you, this town shall be toppled to the ground;
You shall be dumped upside down, deep into the abyss,
Buried within the bowels of the black earth,
And all alike shall lose the life they hold dear."
This speech sprang abroad, and was spread on all sides   365
To burghers in their big halls and bachelors in service;
Such terror overtook them, such torments of dread
That their faces went white, and woe clutched their hearts.
Yet he ceased not his sermoning, but said ever alike:
"God's vengeance verily shall devastate this place."   370
Then the citizens fell silent and sank into grief,
And for dread of God's doom despaired in heart.
Harsh hair-shirts they hauled out, hateful to feel,
And these they bound to their backs and to their bare sides,
Dropped dust on their heads, and dully besought   375
That their pains might please Him who would punish their crimes.

And ever he cries in that country till the king heard
And he rose then and there and ran from his throne
Ripped his royal raiment right off his back,
And huddled with bowed head in a heap of ashes.   380
He asks for a hair shirt and hastily dons it,
Sewed sackcloth thereon, sighing for grief;
Lay dejected in the dust, let the tears drop down,
Bewailing wondrous bitterly all his bad deeds.
Then he said to his sergeants, "Set out in haste   385
To declare this decree, devised by myself:
All beings that draw breath within the bounds of this place,
Males and their animals, females and children,
Each prince, each priest, each prelate as well,
Shall fast henceforth for their foul deeds.   390
Let no babe suck the breast, be it healthy or sick,
Nor beast bite the broom plant or the bent grass either,
Or be put out to pasture, or pull the rich herbs,
Nor shall the ox have his hay, nor the horse have water.
We shall crowd all our starved strength into one cry   395
Whose power shall pierce his heart whose pity shall save us.
Who can predict or presume what will please that Lord
Who governs so graciously in His glory on high?
Though we gravely have grieved Him, his godhead is great:
His mood may melt to mildness, and mercy ensue.   400
And if we veer from our vile ways and divest us of sin,
And pursue the very path He points out Himself,
He will tame His distemper, and turn from His wrath,
And forgive us our guilt, if we grant that he is God."
Then all believed in God's law, and left their sins;   405
Performed fully the penance that the prince advised,
And God in His goodness forgave as foretold:
Though He had otherwise vowed, withheld His vengeance.
Much sorrow then settles on the soul of Jonah;
Anger against his God engulfs him like a storm;   410
Such fury has filled him, he fervently calls
A prayer of complaint to the Prince above:
"I beseech you now, Sire, yourself be the judge:
Were they not my words that forewarned of this change,
That I said when you summoned me to sail from Judea   415
To travel to this town and teach them your will?
I knew well your courteous ways, your wise forbearance,
Your abounding beneficence, the bounty of your grace,
Your leniency, your longsuffering, your delayed vengeance;
And ever mercy in full measure, though the misdeed be huge.   420

I knew well, when I had wielded such words as I could
To menace all these mighty men, the masters of this place,
That for a prayer and a penance you would pardon them all,
And therefore I would have fled far off into Tarshish.
Now, Lord, take my life, it lasts too long;   425
Deal me my death-blow, be done with me at last,
For it seems to me sweeter to cease here and now
Than teach men your message that makes me a liar."
Then a sound from our Sovereign assailed his ears,
As he takes the man to task with trenchant words: 430
"Hark, friend, is it fair so fiercely to rage
For any deed or decree I have dealt you as yet?"
Jonah all joyless, dejected and grumbling,
Goes out to the east of the high-walled city;
He looks around the land for some likely place   435
To wait in and watch what would happen after.
There he built him a bower, the best that he could,
Fashioned of hay and fern, and a few herbs,
For no groves grew on that ground whose green-clad boughs
Could give shelter or shade in the shimmering heat.   440
So he sat in his little booth, his back to the sun,
And soon fell asleep there, and slumbered all night
While God of His grace made grow from that soil
A green vine, the goodliest a gardener could boast.
When God turned dark to dawn and daylight returned,   445
He wakened under woodbine and was well-pleased:
He looked up at the leaves, that lightly moved:
In a lovelier leaf-hall no lodger e'er dwelt,
For the walls were wide apart, arched well above;
Sealed on either side, as snug as a house;   450
An entry-nook on the north, and nowhere else,
All closed around like a copse that casts a cool shade.
He gazed up at the green leaves that graced his bower,
Where breezes ever blew, so blithe and so cool.
Though the sun glared grimly, no glint of its rays   455
Could pierce the sheltering shade to shine there within.
So glad is this guest of his gay lodging
That he lounges there at ease, looking toward town;
Lazing and lolling in the lee of his vine—
As for his diet that day, let the devil take it!   460
And he laughed with delight as he looked all about,
And wished with all his heart that he had such a place
High on Mount Ephraim or Hermon's hill:
"I never hoped to own a more honorable dwelling!"

And when darkness drew on, and desire to sleep,   465
He slipped into slumber, slow under leaves,
While a worm, as God willed, laid waste the root,
And when next he awakened, his woodbine was no more.
Then the Watcher of the winds bade the west blow soft,
And warm the world well with the sweet sighs of Zephyr,   470
That no cloud-shape might shadow the clear-shining sun,
Whose broad face broke forth and blazed like a candle.
When the man roused at morning from the maze of his dreams
He saw well that his woodbine was woefully marred—
All blighted and blasted, those beauteous leaves: 475
The hot sun had harmed them or ever he knew.
Now the heat rose relentless and raged like a fire:
The warm wind from the west withered every plant
Till he perished, or nearly, for hiding-place was none;
His woodbine was bereft him; he wept for sorrow   480
And, overcome with anger, indignantly he calls:
"Ah, you maker of man, what mastery is this,
To afflict so with ill fortune your faithful servant?
Mischiefs of your making mock me evermore.
The sole solace vouchsafed me was soon snatched away: 485
My thrice-blessèd woodbine that blocked out the sun.
But I see that all my sorrows are sent at your command.
So lay the last stroke on me—I live too long."
And God, hearing his grievance, again gave answer:
"Is this right, rash man, all your unruly speech,   490
Vainly for a mere vine to vent so your spleen?
Why suffer such sorrow for something so little?"
"It is not little," said Jonah, "but more like justice.
Would I were out of this world, away under ground!"
"Then consider this, sir, since so sore you are vexed: 495
If I would help my own handiwork, how is that strange?
You lament loud and long over your lost vine,
And never took an hour's time to tend or maintain it,
It was here and went away in the wink of an eye,
Yet so ill-pleased you are, you loathe your own life.   500
Then chide me not if I choose to cherish my work
And pity those poor penitents, their pains and their cries.
First, I molded them of matter I myself had made,
Then watched over them a while, and steered well their course;
And if now at long last I should lose my labor   505
And plunge them into the pit when they are purged of sin,
Sorrow for so sweet a place would sink in my heart:
So many cruel men there are mourning their crimes;

And some are dull dunces who cannot discern
The step from the steep pole of a standing ladder,   510
Or say what secret rule sustains the right hand
In its link with the left, though their lives were at stake.
[And there are some beside these who deserve not to die,][8]
Such as infants in arms that are innocent still,
And light-headed ladies who lack wit to tell   515
The one hand from the other, for all this wide world;
And there are many dumb beasts in barn and in field
Who never sinned in any season, nor were sorry after.
Why rush to revenge me, since some will repent
And come and call me king and acknowledge my words?   520
Were I as hasty as you here, much harm had been done;
Could I forbear no better than you, few souls would be safe.
I may not deal such a doom and be deemed a mild Lord,
For the power to punish must be paired with mercy."
Then be not so ungracious, man—go on your way;   525
Be patient and prudent in pain and in joy,
For he who in ill temper takes to tearing his clothes
Is the sorrier beset as he sews them together.
So, when poverty oppresses me, and pains are strong,
I must ally me with longsuffering, and live without strife,   530
For penance and pain make it plain to see
That patience is a great virtue, though vexing it prove.

Amen.

Notes: *Patience*

1. line 11: **Eight blessings in order.** The Beatitudes; see "Introduction" (p. 83) and "Biblical Sources" (p. 105).
2. line 25: **They . . . who hold their peace.** In the most familiar version of the Bible, the Authorized or "King James," the seventh Beatitude reads "the peace-makers." The meaning of *pacifici*, or "the peaceful ones," in the Latin Bible was sometimes taken to include "the keepers of peace within themselves"; this sort of peacekeeping would of course include remaining silent. I have kept the wording of the original, which meant in the poet's time, and still means, "who keep quiet."
3. line 27: **Who guide well and govern their hearts.** The Latin version of the eighth Beatitude reads "who suffer persecution" (see "Introduction," p. 81). The poet adapts this as "who can steer, [i.e., control] their hearts," referring to self-possession, that is, patience, in suffering.
4. lines 101–8. See "A Note on the Embarcation (Lines 101–8)," p. 88.
5. line 133: **Eurus and Aquilon, east-dwelling winds.** The poet imagines a convergence of two winds on the ship, one from the southeast (Eurus) and the other from the northeast (Aquilon). Two probable sources of these names in the poet's

reading were the descriptions of destructive storms in Acts 27 and in Virgil's *Aeneid*, book I. The violent wind that first cripples Paul's ship in Acts is called "Euroaquilo"; in the *Aeneid*, Eurus and Aquilo are among the winds loosed by Aeolus on Aeneas' fleet. Each of these passages contains descriptive details similar to those in *Patience*.

6. lines 165–67: **Vernagu . . . Diana . . . Neptune . . . Mohammed and Magog.** Characteristically, the poet fleshes out the spare Old Testament account with an abundance of detail, supplying a list of miscellaneous non-Christian divinities. In the Book of Jonah, the narrator simply says that Jonah's shipmates "prayed to their god" (the poet's copy of the Bible may have had the plural form *gods*). Vernagu comes from the medieval Charlemagne epics; Diana and Neptune, from Roman mythology. I have substituted *Magog* for the poet's *Mergot*, which is thought to be a corrupt form of *Magog* in the medieval romances; Magog appears, with Satanic associations, in the biblical books of Ezekiel and Revelation. The invocation of *Mohammed* is an amusing anachronism, which the poet apparently overlooked; the story of Jonah is part of Old Testament, pre-Christian, history, whereas Mohammed came after Jesus, founding a faith that was viewed in medieval times as a heretical departure from Christianity.

7. line 188: **Ragnel in shackles.** In Middle English, the word *ragnel* was used both to mean "devil" and as the name of a devil; devils were laden with chains as a sign of their subordination to God's power.

8. line 513: [**And there are some beside these who deserve not to die.**] I have devised and inserted this line to solve a problem presented by the text of the poem as it stands. Throughout, the lines fall naturally into groups of four; they are in fact printed as four-line stanzas by one modern editor, though this in my view distracts the reader's eye from the continuity of the narrative. But in the single extant manuscript of the poem, there is an anomalous group of three lines corresponding to my lines 510–12. There is also a problem of logical sequence: in God's list of those living in Niniveh whom he had no reason to be angry with, the "dull dunces," referred to in line 507, are more clearly exemplified by people who can't tell the rung of a ladder from the upright, and don't know their left hand from their right (511–13 in the manuscript), than by infants and "light-headed ladies" (508–10). I therefore follow Malcolm Andrew and Ronald Waldron's edition of *The Poems of the Pearl Manuscript* (University of Exeter Press, 1996) in reversing the order of the two passages. But this leaves the relative clause "who cannot tell the rung of a ladder from the upright" without a governing noun or pronoun. I conclude that a line is missing from the manuscript; my conjectural restoration both supplies the grammatically necessary antecedent and makes the pattern of four-line stanzas consistent throughout the poem, which then proves to be 532 rather than 531 lines long.

Biblical Sources

1. The Beatitudes

Matthew 5.3–10

3. Blessed are the poor in spirit: for theirs is the kingdom of heaven.

4. Blessed are the meek: for they shall possess the land.

5. Blessed are they that mourn: for they shall be comforted.

6. Blessed are they that hunger and thirst after justice: for they shall have their fill.

7. Blessed are the merciful: for they shall obtain mercy.

8. Blessed are the clean of heart: for they shall see God.

9. Blessed are the peacemakers: for they shall be called the children of God.

10. Blessed are they that suffer persecution for justice' sake: for theirs is the kingdom of heaven.

Luke 6.20–23

20. . . . Blessed are ye poor, for yours is the kingdom of God.

21. Blessed are ye that hunger now: for you shall be filled. Blessed are ye that weep now: for you shall laugh.

22. Blessed shall you be when men shall hate you, and when they shall separate you, and shall reproach you . . .

23. Be glad in that day and rejoice; for behold, your reward is great in heaven. . . .

2. The Book of Jonah

Chapter 1

1. Now the word of the Lord came to Jonas the son of Amathi, saying:

2. Arise, and go to Ninive the great city, and preach in it: for the wickedness thereof is come up before me.

3. And Jonas rose up to flee into Tharsis from the face of the Lord, and he went down to Joppe, and found a ship going to Tharsis: and he paid the fare thereof, and went down into it, to go with them to Tharsis from the face of the Lord.

4. But the Lord sent a great wind into the sea: and a great tempest was raised in the sea, and the ship was in danger to be broken.

5. And the mariners were afraid, and the men cried to their god: and

they cast forth the wares that were in the ship, into the sea, to lighten it of them: and Jonas went down into the inner part of the ship, and fell into a deep sleep.

6. And the shipmaster came to him, and said to him: Why art thou fast asleep? rise up, and call upon thy God, if so be that God will think of us, that we may not perish.

7. And they said every one to his fellow: Come, and let us cast lots, that we may know why this evil is upon us. And they cast lots, and the lot fell upon Jonas.

8. And they said to him: Tell us for what cause this evil is upon us, what is thy business? of what country art thou? and whither goest thou? or of what people art thou?

9. And he said to them: I am a Hebrew, and I fear the Lord the God of heaven, who made both the sea and the dry land.

10. And the men were greatly afraid, and they said to him: Why hast thou done this? (for the men knew that he fled from the face of the Lord: because he had told them.)

11. And they said to him: What shall we do to thee, that the sea may be calm to us? for the sea flowed and swelled.

12. And he said to them: Take me up, and cast me into the sea, and the sea shall be calm to you: for I know that for my sake this great tempest is upon you.

13. And the men rowed hard to return to land, but they were not able: because the sea tossed and swelled upon them.

14. And they cried to the Lord and said: We beseech thee, O Lord, let us not perish for this man's life, and lay not upon us innocent blood: for thou, O Lord, hast done as it pleased thee.

15. And they took Jonas, and cast him into the sea, and the sea ceased from raging.

16. And the men feared the Lord exceedingly, and sacrificed victims to the Lord, and made vows.

Chapter 2

1. Now the Lord prepared a great fish to swallow up Jonas: and Jonas was in the belly of the fish three days and three nights.

2. And Jonas prayed to the Lord his God out of the belly of the fish.

3. And he said: I cried out of my affliction to the Lord, and he heard me: I cried out of the belly of hell, and thou hast heard my voice.

4. And thou hast cast me forth into the deep in the heart of the sea, and a flood hath compassed me: all thy billows, and thy waves have passed over me.

5. And I said: I am cast away out of the sight of thy eyes: but yet I shall see thy holy temple again.

6. The waters compassed me about even to the soul: the deep hath closed round about, the sea hath covered my head.

7. I went down to the lowest parts of the mountains: the bars of the earth have shut me up for ever: and thou wilt bring up my life from corruption, O Lord my God.

8. When my soul was in distress within me, I remembered the Lord: that my prayer may come to thee, unto thy holy temple.

-   9. They that are vain observe vanities, forsake their own mercy.

10. But I with the voice of praise will sacrifice to thee; I will pay whatsoever I have vowed for my salvation to the Lord.

11. And the Lord spoke to the fish: and it vomited out Jonas upon the dry land.

Chapter 3

1. And the word of the Lord came to Jonas the second time, saying:

2. Arise, and go to Ninive the great city: and preach in it the preaching that I bid thee.

3. And Jonas arose, and went to Ninive, according to the word of the Lord: now Ninive was a great city of three days' journey.

4. And Jonas began to enter into the city one day's journey: and he cried, and said: Yet forty days, and Ninive shall be destroyed.

5. And the men of Ninive believed in God; and they proclaimed a fast, and put on sackcloth from the greatest to the least.

6. And the word came to the king of Ninive; and he rose up out of his throne, and cast away his robe from him, and was clothed with sackcloth, and sat in ashes.

7. And he caused it to be proclaimed and published in Ninive from the mouth of the king and of his princes, saying: Let neither men nor beasts, oxen nor sheep, taste any thing: let them not feed, nor drink water.

8. And let men and beasts be covered with sackcloth, and cry to the Lord with all their strength, and let them turn every one from his evil way, and from the iniquity that is in their hands.

9. Who can tell if God will turn, and forgive: and will turn away from his fierce anger, and we shall not perish?

10. And God saw their works, that they were turned from their evil way: and God had mercy with regard to the evil which he had said that he would do to them, and he did it not.

Chapter 4

1. And Jonas was exceedingly troubled, and was angry:

2. And he prayed to the Lord, and said: I beseech thee, O Lord, is not this what I said, when I was yet in my own country? therefore I went before

to flee into Tharsis: for I know that thou art a gracious and merciful God, patient, and of much compassion, and easy to forgive evil.

3. And now, O Lord, I beseech thee take my life from me: for it is better for me to die than to live.

4. And the Lord said: Dost thou think thou hast reason to be angry?

5. Then Jonas went out of the city, and sat toward the east side of the city: and he made himself a booth there, and he sat under it in the shadow, till he might see what would befall the city.

6. And the Lord God prepared an ivy, and it came up over the head of Jonas, to be a shadow over his head, and to cover him (for he was fatigued): and Jonas was exceeding glad of the ivy.

7. But God prepared a worm, when the morning arose on the following day: and it struck the ivy and it withered.

8. And when the sun was risen, the Lord commanded a hot and burning wind: and the sun beat upon the head of Jonas, and he broiled with the heat: and he desired for his soul that he might die, and said: It is better for me to die than to live.

9. And the Lord said to Jonas: Dost thou think thou hast reason to be angry, for the ivy? And he said: I am angry with reason even unto death.

10. And the Lord said: Thou art grieved for the ivy, for which thou hast not laboured, nor made it to grow, which in one night came up, and in one night perished.

11. And shall I not spare Ninive, that great city, in which there are more than a hundred and twenty thousand persons that know not how to distinguish between their right hand and their left, and many beasts?

Pearl

Introduction

Pearl, like *Patience*, was written by a devout Christian at a time when the Christian church was also the Catholic Church. It is a poem of doctrinal instruction in time of bereavement, rich in allusions to the Psalms, the Gospels, and the Apocalypse, or Book of Revelation. (The most important of these passages are printed in "Biblical Sources," pages 163ff.)

In the opening section of the poem, the narrator visits the place where his pearl dropped to the ground and falls asleep on the plot of earth where she lies buried. He sees in a dream a maiden on the far side of a stream, and immediately recognizes her as his lost pearl. In the ensuing dialogue between them, an important theme emerges, namely, patience, or rather, impatience, linking *Pearl* with its sister poem—the narrator resemblers Jonah in *Patience* in rebelling against God's will. The pearl-maiden tells the dreamer that it is useless for him to lament his earthly loss, behaving like a wounded deer that flings itself wildly about:

> Better to cross yourself, and bless
> The name of the Lord, whatever he send;
> No good can come of your willfulness;
> Who bears bad luck must learn to bend.
> Though like a stricken doe, my friend,
> You plunge and bray, with loud lament,
> This way and that, yet in the end
> As he decrees, you must consent.   (VI.4)*

With this we may compare the narrator's advice to himself in *Patience*, lines 7–8: "Then better for me to bear the brunt as it befalls / Than harp on my hardships, though my heart mislike."

The Story

The story of the poem, on its most literal level, is easy to follow. As it opens, the narrator mourns a pearl of supreme value, and we soon realize that the terms in which he is describing it apply not only to a precious gem, but to

---

* Roman numerals refer to sections and Arabic numerals to stanzas within sections.

a girl. His "secret pearl" has slipped from him into the ground; sweet herbs and spice plants have sprung up where it is buried. The bereaved man visits the spice garden, where he gives way to inconsolable grief and at last falls into a deep swoon. As his body lies asleep, his soul is transported to a resplendent landscape of unearthly beauty. Here he wanders about, his grief forgotten, but soon his way is blocked by a river that he wants above all else to cross, for the country beyond it is even more lovely than that on the nearer side—Paradise, he thinks, must surely be there. As he searches for a ford, he sees on the other side of the river a being who is at once a "child" and a "maiden" of stately bearing, dressed in royal robes and wearing a magnificent crown. Her dress is wholly white, adorned with many pearls; a single pearl of great price lies upon her breast. The sight of her stabs his heart, for he recognizes her as one he once knew well, who was "nearer to him than aunt or niece." The apparition comes down the shore on the other side of the river and greets him graciously. He hails her in return as his lost lamented pearl, but then elicits from her the first of a series of rebukes by complaining that she, lost to him, dwells in bliss while he is left to mourn.

This speech and the pearl-maiden's answer initiate a conversation between the two that takes up most of the rest of the poem. We know the narrator to be a Christian; even in his grief at the outset, he expresses his awareness of the "nature of Christ" and the comfort that is, at least theoretically, to be derived from it. But his knowledge of doctrine seems not to be matched by understanding, and the pearl-maiden must dispel a number of misapprehensions on his part. He cannot understand why he may not cross the stream and join her in blessedness forthwith. He does not see how she can be a queen in heaven when that rank is held by Mary; no one could take Mary's crown from her who did not surpass her in some respect, yet Mary is "singular," peerless, like the Phoenix. He finds it unjust that royal rank should have been bestowed on one whose accomplishments in life were negligible, who did not live two years on earth and could not even say her prayers or recite the creed. To resolve this last difficulty, the pearl-maiden tells him the New Testament parable of the vineyard (Matthew 20), according to which the owner of the vineyard pays each laborer the same wage, a single penny, for his day's work, no matter how late the hour at which it began; the owner of the vineyard stands for God, and the "penny" is eternal life in the heavenly kingdom. But this in turn baffles the dreamer. The equal wage is unreasonable, he says, and what is more, it contradicts a statement in the Bible which he can quote, that God "renders unto every man according to his work" (Psalm 61.13 [A.V. 62.12]).

At this point (and it is also the halfway point of the poem), the pearl-maiden's exposition shifts its emphasis from justice and right to grace and mercy. All men, as a result of Adam's disobedience to God, are born in sin and condemned to physical death and then to the second death of everlasting damnation. But Adam's guilt was redeemed by the voluntary death of Christ, which also expressed God's boundless love for humankind. The blood that ran from the pierced side of Christ on the Cross symbolizes redemption, and the water that came with it signifies the sacrament of baptism, administered by the Church, which brings redemption to the individual soul. A baptized child who dies in infancy has, it is true, done no works of righteousness, but neither has it sinned, whereas the best of men sin constantly and must repeatedly be returned to a state of grace through contrition and penance. The dead infant is an "innocent"—literally, one who has done no harm; the claim of such spotless souls to the bliss of heaven is wholly in accord with reason and indeed is clearer than that of the righteous man.

The pearl-maiden has spoken sternly, and she has matched the dreamer's quotation from the Psalms with another, more threatening one, to the effect that no man shall be justified in the sight of the Lord (Psalm 142.2 [A.V. 143]). Her tone now changes as she speaks of the tenderness of the living Jesus, who invited the little children to come to him. The figure of the child unspotted by sin knocking at the gate of the kingdom of heaven, which will open straightway to receive him, opens a new phase in the development of the poem in which materials from the Old Testament, the Gospels, and the Book of Revelation, as interpreted in early church tradition, are woven together in language of unsurpassed intensity and power. The pearl now enters for the first time in its major symbolic role as the "one pearl of great price" in the parable told by Jesus in the Gospel of Matthew, for which the merchant seeking goodly pearls sold all he had. The maiden explains that the pearl is like the heavenly kingdom; it is spotless, like the souls of the innocent; it is perfectly round and thus "endless," like eternity; it is "blithe" and thus represents the bliss of the redeemed.

Endlessness here does not mean "infinite continuance," as the modern reader might think. Rather, eternity means freedom from measurements of time, as the circumference of a circle is free from interruptions, that is, from beginnings and ends. In the parable of the vineyard, it is significant that the penny symbolizing the heavenly reward is circular in form, and that in some interpretations of the parable it was identified with the communion wafer, also circular. Communion, for the faithful Christian, prefigures oneness with the divine in eternal happiness. Because this reward, for all who receive it, is "beyond price," comparative values such as "first" and "last," "higher" and "lower," have no meaning within it. The pearl of great price is, in fact, the "one pure pearl" visible on the maiden's breast, bestowed upon her by the Lamb at the time of their wedding in token of the peace of heaven and the spotlessness for which he loved her.

Just as the dreamer had supposed that there could be only one queen in heaven, so he now supposes that the pearl-maiden, in becoming the bride of the Lamb, must have been preferred to all others, including many women who had lived and died for Christ in saintly fashion. But the maiden, carefully distinguishing between two similar words in Middle English, explains that while she is indeed spotless (*maskeles*, or immaculate), she is not unique (*makeles*, or matchless). She reveals herself to be one of the 144,000 virgins seen with the Lamb on Mount Sion in the New Jerusalem by St. John the Divine and described by him in the Book of Revelation. These in turn were identified in medieval tradition with the Holy Innocents whose martyrdom is commemorated yearly by the church—the children under the age of two whom Herod killed, thinking thus to kill the infant Jesus. The pearl-maiden, who did not live two years on earth, has joined this celestial company. The bridegroom to whom all of them alike are wedded, and with whom they live in joy, is the Lamb of God, invoked by Isaiah in the Old Testament as he that takes away the sins of the world, condemned to death by the Jews in Jerusalem and crucified there, and seen in heaven beside the throne of God by St. John the Divine.

This exposition gives rise to another misunderstanding on the dreamer's part. The pearl-maiden has told him that she lives with the Lamb, but that cannot be in "Jerusalem," for she is there on the other side of the river and Jerusalem is on earth, in the kingdom of Judea. This confusion in turn is resolved by the maiden, who distinguishes between the Old Jerusalem, where the trial and crucifixion of Christ took place, and the New Jerusalem, seen descending out of heaven by St. John (Revelation 21). In accordance with the traditional interpretations of the name *Jerusalem* as "city of God" and "sight of peace," this latter is the city where the souls of the blessed, once their bodies have suffered earthly death and decay, dwell with God in eternal harmony and rest.

The request the dreamer now makes, as he speaks for the last time, poignantly reflects his love for the maiden in her former condition as a human child. He wants, he says, to see the place where she lives, the great city and the "blissful bower," the wedding chamber, within it. Here, late in the unfoldment of the narrative as also in *Sir Gawain and the Green Knight*, we learn what has set the entire sequence of events in motion, beginning with the narrator's swoon over the mound in the herb garden. The pearl-maiden tells him that no mortal may enter the celestial city, but that "through great favor" she has obtained permission from the Lamb for him to see it from the outside. She has, that is, interceded for him that he may be brought out of his spiritual impasse, mediating between him and God, as the saints, when men pray to them, are thought to do. Beneath her seemingly impersonal, if not cold, attitude toward him during much of their conversation lies the loving concern implicit in this act.

The description of the celestial Jerusalem, seen by the dreamer across the river from a hill to which the pearl-maiden has directed him, follows closely—much of the time almost word for word—the description in the Book of Revelation, as if the poet wished thereby to insist on the authenticity of the vision. There are the twelve foundations, each made of a single precious stone; the cubic shape as St. John saw it measured; the twelve pearly gates; the golden streets; and, within the city, the throne of God and the elders seated around it. Then, as, on earth, the risen full moon begins to shine in the east while it is still daylight (such is the poem's unforgettable simile), the dreamer becomes aware of a procession moving toward the throne, led by the Lamb and made up of the thousands upon thousands of his brides. All are dressed as the pearl-maiden had been dressed; all wear the pearl of great price. In a moment of all but unbearable poignancy, he sees among the others in the procession his "little queen." As he recognizes her, the entrancement of spiritual vision gives way to that delight in the sight of the beloved that for earthly beings is inseparable from the desire to possess. He rushes toward the river, determined to cross it, come what may, and wakens from his dream.

Symbolism and Theme

Such is the density of symbolic meaning in *Pearl* that the story of the poem, maiden and all, has sometimes been interpreted wholly in allegorical terms. But the force of certain details seems clearly circumstantial, pointing toward the story of an individual man as much as to that of the Christian soul in general, and the commonsense view has prevailed in more recent criticism: that the poem is at once autobiographical and allegorical, founded on an actual experience of bereavement and dealing with that experience in terms of Christian symbols and doctrine.

Another question of interpretation has to do with the so-called obtuseness of the dreamer. It is implausible (the argument runs) that he, a professed Christian, should not already understand the doctrinal points the maiden is making, should keep asking virtually the same question again and again. But his persistent wrongheadedness makes sense if we consider how deeply founded it is in the limitations of the mortal perspective. Seeing the pearl-maiden standing on the other side of a river, he naturally concludes that she is "there" in the same sense in which another person would be there, a certain distance away, in life. Actually, the dreamed encounter by the river, within speaking range, symbolizes the maiden's role as an intermediary between the dreamer and the heavenly realm to which he does not belong. Even as the maiden speaks to him, one is tempted to say, she is in the procession moving through the streets of the celestial Jerusalem in the company of the Lamb, as the dreamer sees her to be at the end of the poem. Yet the procession itself, like the marriage relationship, is a symbol of spiritual union, the visible for the invisible. Such questions as "Where is she really?" "What is she really doing?" have no answer, indeed no meaning, on this plane.

So too with the pearl. At the beginning of the poem, it stands for what has been most precious to the narrator in this world—in Shakespeare's words, there where he has garnered up his heart. Seeing the maiden, recognizing her (so it seems) as the very being he so loves, the dreamer naturally thinks that what he has found is what he had lost. He does not and at this stage cannot realize that his earthly pearl has passed into another mode of existence. All that was truly precious in her is now forever merged in the transcendent values of the heavenly kingdom. She can be possessed only by possessing that, and that can be possessed only by giving up the things of this world, as the merchant sold all he had to obtain the one pearl of the parable.

But between earthly and divine orders there is a separation that cannot be bridged by the unaided efforts of the human mind. The characteristics of the pearl as the maiden describes them in telling the parable of the merchant are signs of this radical discontinuity. Having the form of a circle, the pearl, as we have already observed, stands for eternity, the existence of God in a timeless present from the perspective of which human history is a completed, static pattern. Human beings are trapped in progressive time, looking back from the present to the past and forward to an unknown future. Eternity is not perpetual duration, "longer than" time; it is the absence of time. So too with the worth of the heavenly pearl. It is not "greater than" the worth of anything on earth; it is absolute, literally "beyond measure." Nearer and farther, earlier and later, lower and higher, less and more—all are interdependent manifestations of a dimensional mode of being in which men, under the governance of changing fortune, move toward certain death. "We look before and after, And pine for what is not": the inner dissatisfaction and perpetual striving inevitable in such a world have their otherworldly counterparts in the peace of heaven. To dwell there is to possess a happiness that, again, is not "greater than" human happiness, but perfect, without qualification.

From this disparity arise all the paradoxes and contradictions that baffle the dreamer so. That everyone in heaven is a king or queen; that the "penny" of eternal life, the wage of everyone who works in the vineyard, has no relation to comparative deserts; that everyone in heaven has the same reward "no matter how little or great his gains" (XI.1)—such statements cannot be understood in commonsense, "realistic" terms. They are attempts to express in language what language was not designed to express.

The dreamer, for all that he is transported to a "place" of visionary enlightenment, cannot escape the earthly habit of comparative measurement. *More*, in fact, is the link word of two sections of the poem: in section III, at the beginning of the dream, where, released from sorrow, the dreamer experiences a joy that intensifies until he is brought to a halt at the river, and in section X, where the laborers who came earliest to the vine want their wages commensurately increased. In section XV, when the maiden is telling of her life in heaven as a bride of the Lamb, the link-word is *nevertheless*;

the word *more*, which appears twice in stanza 1, now signifies values that exceed human imagining. The dream breaks off because the dreamer, having been granted a sight of his pearl in its heavenly setting, wants something more and rushes into the stream to attain it. Reproaching himself after he has awakened, he reflects ruefully that "always men would have and hoard / And gain the more, the more they get" (XX.4).

Yet the experience of the dream does change him, and the evolution of his attitudes and feelings in the course of the poem breathes dramatic life into what would otherwise have been unrelieved didacticism. At first, as we saw, he is querulous and self-centered, then brash and presumptuous in assuming that he and the glorious personage on the other side of the river exist on the same plane. For this latter misapprehension he receives her coldest rebuke. But then he takes an important step: forsaking his obstinacy and confessing his foolishness, he throws himself on God's mercy in a kind of self-administered baptism (VII.1):

> As water flows from a fountainhead
> I cast myself in his mercy clear.

More important, he stops thinking solely about what he has suffered and what he desires, and begins to sense his own ignorance about what it is he is seeing. The question he asks, "What is your life?" (VII.3), has, at the moment of asking, profounder implications than he or we realize. The answer, it turns out, is life itself—in terms of Christian doctrine, the life beyond mortality compared to which life as we know it is a continual dying. By the time the maiden has expounded the parable of the vineyard and justified the place in heaven of the innocent, the dreamer is filled with awe, overwhelmed by her angelic aspect and more than earthly magnificence even as he remains still wrongheaded, still trying to understand her heavenly station in terms of what he knows. His last request is made with the utmost reverence and humility, though it too is humanly motivated, reflecting the same partiality which leads at last to his ill-fated attempt to cross the river.

What, in the end, has he learned? We have already heard his self-admonishment in the concluding section. If, he thinks, he had been less impatient, more willing to be content with what had been granted him, he would not have been banished so soon from the country of his vision. But this facile moralizing hardly addresses the problem of his initial despair, and a far deeper lesson is implicit in the terms of his farewell to the pearl-maiden (XX.3).

> Then sorrow broke from my burning breast;
> "O honored Pearl," I said, "how dear
> Was your every word and wise behest
> In this true vision vouchsafed me here.
> If you in a garland never sere

Are set by that Prince all-provident,
Then happy am I in dungeon drear
That he with you is well content."

In the symbol of the garland, a completed circle, we see an intimation of eternity on the speaker's part. The disparity between garland and dungeon further suggests his realization that the mortal and immortal realms are closed off from each other, that the "distance" between the two cannot be crossed as if it were a river. It is significant that nowhere in the final stanzas does he speak of his hope to be reunited with his pearl in heaven, or of his anticipation of that reunion, in expressing his reconcilement to his earthly lot. The deepest lesson he has been taught is an imaginative apprehension of what his lost pearl now is, part of an everlasting and changeless order. Such a garland, unlike one made of earthly flowers, cannot fade, nor can the man lose it who has learned to value it properly. Knowing this, and grateful for the grace that has accorded him the enlightening vision, the speaker commits to God his pearl and his poem, calling down upon both the blessing of Christ and praying that all men may be made conformable to the divine will.

The Literary Background

We have so far seen *Pearl* exclusively in relation to the Bible and Christian tradition. But it is an imaginative, as well as a doctrinal, work, and we must therefore say something about its literary background as well. Knowing little or nothing about the author's life, we cannot attempt a full account of influences and sources as we might for a Yeats or a Stevens. But it is obvious that *Pearl* shares important elements of theme and dramatic presentation with two major literary works that were so widely read in the Middle Ages that the poet would inevitably have known them: *The Consolation of Philosophy* and *The Romance of the Rose*.

The Consolation of Philosophy, like *Pearl*, has its point of departure in the circumstances and mental state of its narrator. Boethius, who lived in the late fifth and early sixth centuries, was thrown into prison and finally executed after having enjoyed prosperity and power under the Roman emperor Theodoric. At the beginning of the *Consolation* he speaks as a captive, complaining of the conditions in which he finds himself, unable to reconcile himself to the loss of his former good fortune. He is visited by a feminine being of supernatural majesty whom he belatedly recognizes as Philosophy, the "nurse of his youth." There follows a lengthy conversation between the two in which the prisoner's role is largely passive. Philosophy rebukes him for his despair and consoles him by gradually leading him to a full under-

standing of the relationship between transitory and lasting goods. The former
are the gifts to men on earth of the changeable goddess Fortuna, who will
inevitably take them away. The latter belong to man's soul, which is also his
rational intelligence; once possessed, they cannot be lost.

The lesson of the *Consolation*, though it is presented in philosophic rather
than religious terms, is much the same as what I have described as the
implicit lesson of *Pearl*. But if the "meaning" of *Pearl* is to this extent Bo-
ethian, the emotional climate of the poem is far otherwise. *Pearl* is not only
a dialogue affording doctrinal enlightenment; it is a dream-vision suffused
with the ardor of what we now call romantic love. In this it resembles that
greatest exemplar of the medieval dream-vision, *The Romance of the Rose*,
a poem we know the *Pearl*-poet had read and admired because he alludes
to it in *Purity*. Written in the first half of the thirteenth century by the
French poet Guillaume de Lorris, the first part of the *Romance* describes a
wonderful dream that begins on a May morning. The youthful narrator (he
is, he tells us, at the age when love rules men's hearts) finds himself in a
delightful landscape, which shares with the dream landscape of *Pearl* such
features as leafy trees and bushes and joyfully singing birds, though these
are more naturalistically described. Wandering about, delighting in the
beauty of the scene, he pauses to bathe his face in a clear stream, then
follows it along its bank. At last he comes to a garden or park surrounded
by a high wall, to which he succeeds in gaining access. Neither the garden
nor its inhabitants, chief among whom is the god of love, need be described
here; more important with relation to *Pearl* is the dreamer's discovery, in
the garden, of a fountain at the bottom of which are two brilliant crystal
stones. He gazes into the fountain and sees reflected there a bush laden with
blooming red roses to which he is immediately attracted. Seen close at hand,
it enraptures him with its sweetness, and one especially beautiful rosebud
becomes the object of his love. The story that follows tells of his frustrated
attempts to gain possession of the rose, but de Lorris did not complete the
poem, and it was continued in more satiric and discursive vein by Jean de
Meun.

The Romance of the Rose is an allegory of love on the human plane. But
the conventional language of secular love poetry in medieval times was also
used in a considerable body of religious poetry addressed to the Virgin Mary.
In *Pearl*, the feelings of a father for his lost infant daughter, who appears to
him as an angelic visitant, are expressed in this same language. As has often
been noted, the maiden has the typical physical attributes of the idealized
mistress—slender figure, gray eyes, hair like gold, flawless complexion—and
the terms in which the dreamer addresses her—"my jewel," "my sweet,"
"my adored one"—are such as a lover would use to his lady. Yet she is also
a virgin and a saint, and other terms applied to her—"special spice," "im-
maculate bride," "immaculate maid so meek and mild"—clearly associ-

ate her with Mary. The educational process dramatized in *Pearl* involves not the negation of human passion but its removal from the realm of mutability—a lifting up of the heart to higher things.

Design and Its Significance

One of the most striking and significant aspects of the poem is its conformity to an all-encompassing and highly elaborated design. Elements of this design are found separately elsewhere, but the intricacy of their combination in *Pearl* is unmatched in English poetry before or since. The twelve-line stanza used by the poet is found in many other Middle English poems on religious subjects; the stanzas of these poems characteristically end in a repeated or varied refrain. The rhyme scheme, *ababababbcbc*, is an extraordinarily difficult one. It requires no fewer than four *a*-rhymes and six *b*-rhymes per stanza, and the repetition of the refrain calls for a number of *c*-rhymes as well. *Pearl* is divided into twenty sections, each of which, with the exception of section XV, contains five stanzas. The last line of each of the five stanzas making up a given section ends in a link-word that is sometimes part of a repeated phrase ("without a spot," "is enough for all"); the same link-word also appears in the first lines of all but one of the five stanzas. The sections themselves are joined by the device of "concatenation," or overlapping repetition: the link-word of a given section appears in the first line of the first stanza of the following section. For example, in the last stanza of section III, the link-word *more* appears in the first and last lines; it makes its final appearance in the first line of the first stanza of section IV, which ends with the new linking phrase "pearls of price":

> The more I mused on that fair face,
> The person of that most precious one,
> Such gladness grew in my heart by grace
> As little before had been, or none.
> I longed to call across that space
> But found my powers of speech had flown;
> To meet her in so strange a place—
> Such a sight, in truth, might shock or stun!
> Then raised she up her brow, that shone
> All ivory pale on that far shore,
> That stabbed my heart to look upon
> And ever the longer, more and more.
>
> More dread diminished my delight;
> I stood stock-still and dared not call.
> With eyes wide open and mouth shut tight
> I hoved there tame as hawk in hall.

> Unearthly, I knew, must be that plight;
> I dreaded much what might befall,
> Lest she I viewed should vanish quite
> And leave me there to stare and stall.
> That slender one, so smooth, so small,
> Unblemished, void of every vice,
> Rose up in robes imperial,
> A precious pearl in pearls of price.

Finally, it is important to note that the link-word of the final section also appears, in rhyming position, in the first line of the first stanza of the poem. The end is thus connected back to the beginning in a kind of temporal circularity. The presence of the statement "I am alpha and omega, the first and the last," in chapters 1 and 22 of the Book of Revelation has been thought to be an instance of this same device. A modern example of both circularity and concatenation is Donne's "La Corona" (The crown), in which each of seven sonnets has as its first line the last line of the preceding one, and the last line of the last is also the first line of the first. The thematic significance of such a pattern in a poem so entitled need scarcely be pointed out, and we are reminded that circularity is also a symbolic attribute of the pearl.

Circularity or roundness is a symbol not only of eternity but of perfection: Philosophy, in the *Consolation*, quotes the ancient philosopher Parmenides to the effect that "the divine essence is 'in body like a sphere, perfectly rounded on all sides.' " Another visible symbol of perfection is symmetry, exemplified most notably in *Pearl* in the shape of the celestial Jerusalem. The poet repeats the description given by St. John, who saw the city measured; it was twelve thousand furlongs in length, breadth, and height, a perfect cube. Symmetry is further exemplified by the outer walls of the city, each with its three gates. The number twelve is the total number of gates, the number of the trees growing beside the river of life, and the base of the city's measurement in furlongs. It is also the number of lines in the stanzas of *Pearl*. The square of a number is a mathematical expression of symmetry, and the square of twelve, multiplied by a thousand, is the number of the virgins accompanying the Lamb. Given these facts, we cannot fail to find it significant that the one hundred and one stanzas of *Pearl* have a total of 1212 lines. But one hundred is also the square of the "perfect number," ten, in which the decimal sequence returns to one plus zero, and the one hundred-and-first stanza of the poem can be thought of as overlapping, and thus coinciding with, the first stanza, to close the circle. Corroborating evidence of the *Pearl*-poet's interest in number and numerical design is found in *Sir Gawain and the Green Knight* (see the "Introduction" to that poem, p. 11).

It is natural for the modern reader to wonder whether all this patterning in *Pearl* is mere display—artifice for artifice's sake. But the very question implies that the answer may be found in the relationship between display and purpose, form and content, or, to use a characteristically medieval analogy often applied to literary works, husk and kernel. Most obviously in the realm of tangible artifacts, painstaking elaboration signifies and confers value. In early times, the hand-copied manuscript was such an artifact; we think of the gorgeously bound and illuminated Bibles, missals, and books of hours whose material worth was a sign that they bore a priceless message. We think too of the medieval reliquary with its profusion of ornament worked in ivory or metal. And these in turn suggest an important group of images in *Pearl:* the jeweler, the jewel, and the enclosing box. The dreamer in section V tells the maiden that since he has been separated from her he has been "a joyless jeweler"; the maiden replies that he is mistaken—his pearl cannot be lost to him when it is enclosed in so comely a "coffer" as the garden in which he sees her. There is a grim pun here, for *coffer* in Middle English could also mean "coffin" (I have substituted *casket*, which has a similar mortuary meaning in American English). The root-meaning of the word *garden* is in fact "enclosed place"; the garden of Eden where Adam and Eve first lived was a bounded precinct, a kind of park. Heaven was commonly visualized as a celestial version of the earthly paradise. Alternatively, it was visualized as a city, the celestial Jerusalem. This latter, having walls, is also a kind of enclosure or box—a coffer, fashioned sumptuously of precious substances, containing the treasure of eternal life. An analogy becomes irresistible: the verbal artifact called *Pearl* is itself a kind of painstakingly crafted container, embellished with every device of language in order that it may be worthy of its contents, the vision of the pearl-maiden and the precious teachings she imparts.

Design in *Pearl* has an additional dimension of significance. Like any literary work, the poem exists temporally rather than spatially; it must be experienced part by part. But having been experienced, it can be contemplated, in terms of its numerical form, its sections, its stanzas, its rhymes, and its metrical patterns, as a patterned object. Moving through time toward a condition of timelessness, the poem fulfills the aspiration it dramatically represents.

The Translation

In translating *Pearl,* I have reproduced the schemes of rhyme, repetition, and concatenation described above; whatever difficulties these present, the poem could scarcely retain its identity without them. I have also followed the poet as best I could in the linking of stressed syllables by initial alliteration, especially in passages of heightened dramatic intensity. Language in these latter is at times loaded with alliteration, consonance, and other linkages among sounds to the point where the shapes of words threaten to become more conspicuous than their sense, and similar effects have found their way into my translation. Lines such as

> His gifts gush forth like a spring in spate
> Or a stream in a gulley that runs in rains, (XI.2)

or

> As in his flock no fleck is seen,
> His hallowed halls are wholly bright, (XVI.3)

may strike the modern reader as overwrought, but they have their counterparts in the poem and would not, I think, have offended the ears to which it was first addressed.

Another kind of verbal extravagance in which *Pearl* abounds is wordplay. The necessity of repeating the link-words leads to the sort of pun that exploits the range of senses of a single word, as when *spot* means both "speck" and "place," *deem* both "express an opinion" and "pronounce sentence," and *right* both "valid claim" and "rectitude." But the *Pearl*-poet did not eschew the lowliest form of wit either. In the original, he substitutes *now* for the link-word *enow* "enough" in XI.2, and in section XVI uses two words of identical form: *mote* "speck" and *mote* "walled city" (related to *moat*). (Elsewhere in the poem he puns on yet another word spelled *mote*, modern *moot*, meaning "debate" of "strife.") He seems to rejoice in the phonetic identity in his dialect of *lamb* and *lamp*, writing "God himself was their lamp-light [the text has the spelling *lombe-lyght*], The Lamb their lantern" (XVIII.2). These homonymic puns cannot be reproduced in modern English, but in view of their presence in the original, I have felt justified in combining *wholly* and *holy* as a link-word in section XVI—a pun that is in fact of the more respectable sort, because the two words go back to a single root.

As for the diction of the translation, I have tried to conform to the original in making it at once traditional and varied. It would not have occurred to the author of *Pearl* to avoid formulaic combinations of words, whether poetic or colloquial, or to think of such combinations as "clichés" in the modern derogatory sense. I have made use of some distinctively literary diction, as the *Pearl*-poet himself did, though I have tried to avoid burned-out archaisms. The occasional echo of Milton, Shakespeare, or the King James Bible, when it suggested itself, was allowed to stay; and stock phrases like "heart's desire," "daily round," "lost and lamented," "royal road," and others have been incorporated as in keeping with the style both of *Pearl* and of *Sir Gawain and the Green Knight*. I have also emulated a complementary effect of diction peculiar to *Pearl*, of the deployment or display of abundant resources. One has the impression that the poet never inadvertently repeats an adjective, a rhyming combination, or even a rhyme sound. Important attributes such as spotlessness, brightness, and happiness seem to be described in endlessly fresh combinations of words, and this aspect of the language offers a particular challenge to the translator, as well as conferring on the poem a richness befitting its character as an artifact.

In *Pearl,* if in any poem, we see the poet offering up his craft, creating expressive power out of the very restrictions imposed on expression. To emulate such an achievement is an act of the greatest temerity, especially because, as with dancing on pointe, the limitations accepted by the artist are justified only insofar as he transcends them. The result of my long labors may or may not be found worthy of comparison with the original; "if not," in the words of Emily Dickinson,

> I had
> The transport of the aim.

Pearl†

I

1

Pearl, that a prince is well content
To give a circle of gold to wear,
Boldly I say, all orient
Brought forth none precious like to her;
So comely in every ornament,   5
So slender her sides, so smooth they were,
Ever my mind was bound and bent
To set her apart without a peer.
In a garden of herbs I lost my dear;[1]
Through grass to ground away it shot;   10
Now, lovesick, the heavy loss I bear
Of that secret pearl without a spot.

2

Since in that spot it sped from me so,
Often I watched and wished for that grace
That once was wont to banish woe   15
And bless with brightness all my days;
That clutches my heart in cruel throe
And causes my blood to rage and race,
Yet sweeter songs could no man know
Than silence taught my ear to trace;   20
And many there came, to think of her face
With cover of clay so coldly fraught:
O earth, you mar a gem past praise,
My secret pearl without a spot.

---

† Notes for *Pearl* appear on pages 161–63.

3

That spot with spice must spring and spread   25
Where riches rotted in narrow room;
Blossoms white and blue and red
Lift now alight in blaze of noon;
Flower and fruit could never fade
Where pearl plunged deep in earthen tomb,   30
For the seed must die to bear the blade
That the wheat may be brought to harvest home.°
Good out of good to all and some:
Such a seed could never have come to nought
Nor spice in splendor spare to bloom   35
From that precious pearl without a spot.

4

To that especial spot I hied
And entered that same garden green
In August at a festive tide
When corn is cut with scythe-edge keen.   40
On the mound where pearl went tumbling wide,
Leaf vied with leaf in shade and sheen:
Gillyflower and ginger on every side
And peonies peerless blooming between.
But fairer yet, and all unseen,   45
Was the fragrance that my senses sought;
There, I know, is the dear demesne
Of my precious pearl without a spot.

5

Before that spot with head inclined
I stretched my hand in stark despair;   50
My heart lamented, deaf and blind,
Though reason reconciled my care.
I mourned my pearl so close confined
With thoughts in throng contending there;
Comfort of Christ might come to mind   55
But wretched will would not forbear.
I fell upon that flower-bed fair;
Such odor seized my brain distraught
I slipped into slumber unaware,
On that precious pearl without a spot.   60

° John 12.24.

II

1

My soul forsook that spot in space
And left my body on earth to bide.
My spirit sped, by God's good grace,
On a quest where marvels multiplied.
I knew not where in the world it was,   65
But I saw I was set where cliffs divide;
A forest flourished in that place
Where many rich rocks might be descried.
The glory that flashed there far and wide
Eye could not credit, nor mind invent;   70
Pure cloth-of-gold were pale beside
Such rich and rare embellishment.

2

Embellished were those hills in view
With crystal cliffs as clear as day
And groves of trees with boles as blue   75
As indigo silks of rich assay;
The leaves, like silver burnished new,
Slide rustling rife on every spray;
As shifts of cloud let sunshine through,
They shot forth light in shimmering play.   80
The gravelstones that strewed the way
Were precious pearls of orient;
The beams of the sun but blind and gray
Beside such bright embellishment.

3

Amid those hills embellished bright   85
My sorrows fled in full retreat;
Fragrance of fruits with great delight
Filled me like food that mortals eat.
Birds of all colors fanned in flight
Their iridescent pinions fleet,   90
But lute or lyre, by craft or sleight,
Could not make music half so sweet,
For while in time their wings they beat
In glad accord their voices blent;

With more of mirth might no man meet   95
Than hear each brave embellishment.

4

So all embellished was the land
Where Fortune bears me on my way;
No tongue is worthy to command
Fit words those splendors to display.   100
I walked along with bliss at hand;
No slope so steep to make me stay;
The further, the fairer the pear trees stand,
The spice-plants spread, the blossoms sway,
And hedgerows run by banks as gay   105
As glittering golden filament;
I came to the shore of a waterway:[2]
Dear God, what brave embellishment!

5

Embellishing those waters deep,
Banks of pure beryl greet my gaze;   110
Sweetly the eddies swirl and sweep
With a rest and a rush in murmuring phrase;
Stones in the stream their colors steep,
Gleaming like glass where sunbeam strays,
As stars, while men of the marshlands sleep,   115
Flash in winter from frosty space;
For every one was a gem to praise,
A sapphire or emerald opulent,
That seemed to set the pool ablaze,
So brilliant their embellishment.   120

III

1

Embellished with such wondrous grace
Were wood and water and shining plain,
My pleasures multiplied apace,
Conquered my cares, dispelled my pain.
By the brink of a river that runs a race   125
Blissful I walked with busy brain;
The more I explored that plashy place
The greater strength did gladness gain.

As proof of Fortune's purpose plain
Makes a man's heart to sink or soar, 130
He whom she plies with bliss or bane
Of what he draws is dealt still more.

2

More of bliss was there to prize
Than ever my tongue could testify,
For earthly heart could not suffice 135
To sustain one tenth of that pure joy.
It could not be but Paradise
Lay beyond those noble banks, thought I,[3]
And the stream itself seemed a device,
A mark to know a boundary by. 140
Those peerless precincts to espy
I need but gain the further shore;
But I dared not wade, for the water ran high,
And longing mastered me more and more.

3

More than ever and ever the more 145
To cross that river was all my care,
For lovely though this landscape were,
What lay beyond was past compare.
I stared about, scanning the shore
For a ford to afford me thoroughfare, 150
But dangers direr than before
Appeared, the more I wandered there.
And still it seemed I should not forbear
For dangers, with delights in store;
But now was broached a new affair 155
My mind was moved by, more and more.

4

More marvels now amazed me quite:
Beyond that stream, strange to behold,
There rose a cliff of crystal bright
With resplendent rays all aureoled. 160
At the foot was seated in plain sight
A maiden child of mortal mold,
A gracious lady gowned in white;
I knew her well, I had seen her of old.

As fine-spun floss of burnished gold, 165
So shone she, peerless, as of yore;
I gazed on her with joy untold,
The longer, I knew her more and more.

5

The more I mused on that fair face,
The person of that most precious one, 170
Such gladness grew in my heart by grace
As little before had been, or none.
I longed to call across that space
But found my power of speech had flown;
To meet her in so strange a place— 175
Such a sight, in truth, might shock or stun!
Then raised she up her brow, that shone
All ivory pale on that far shore,
That stabbed my heart to look upon
And ever the longer, more and more. 180

IV

1

More dread diminished my delight;
I stood stock-still and dared not call.
With eyes wide open and mouth shut tight
I hoved there tame as hawk in hall.
Unearthly, I knew, must be that plight; 185
I dreaded much what might befall,
Lest she I viewed should vanish quite
And leave me there to stare and stall.
That slender one, so smooth, so small,
Unblemished, void of every vice, 190
Rose up in robes imperial,
A precious pearl in pearls of price.

2

Pearls of price in ample store
Were there to see by grace divine
As she, approaching, shone on shore 195
Like fleurs-de-lys to kings condign.

Her surcoat of white linen pure°
Had open sides of fair design,
And filigree on bands it bore
Where lavish pearls their lustre join,   200
And lappets large, with double line
Of pearls set round in that same guise;
Her gown of that same linen fine,
And all bedecked with pearls of price.

3

Her priceless crown with pearls alone   205
Was set, in fashion fit and fair;
High pinnacles upon it shone,
And florets carved with craft and care.
Other headdress had she none
To frame her ivory forehead bare;   210
As earl or duke by royal throne,
So sage she seemed, so grave her air.
About her shoulders fell her hair
Like gold spun fine by artifice,
Whose deepest hue yet had a share   215
Of pallor pure of pearls of price.

4

Pearls of price in rows ornate
On hem, on side, on wristband rest;
No other gem could suit her state
Who was in white so richly dressed.   220
But one pure pearl, a wonder great,
Was set secure upon her breast;
A man might ponder long and late
Ere its full worth were well assessed.
I think no tongue could ever attest   225
A discourteous thought of that device,
So white it was, so wholly blessed,
And proudest placed of pearls of price.

5

In pearls of price she moved at ease
Toward the rim of the river that flowed so free;   230

° Apocalypse 19.7–8 (A.V. Revelation); cf. VII.5.5–6.

No gladder man from here to Greece
Than I, that blessèd sight to see.
She was nearer my heart than aunt or niece:
So much the more my joy must be;
She proffered parley in sign of peace,　　　　235
Bowed womanlike with bended knee,
Took off her crown of high degree
And bade me welcome with courteous voice;
That I was born O well for me
To greet that girl in pearls of price.　　　　240

V

1

"O pearl," said I, in pearls of price,
Are you my pearl come back again,
Lost and lamented with desolate sighs
In darkest night, alone and in vain?
Since you slipped to ground where grasses rise　　　　245
I wander pensive, oppressed with pain,
And you in the bliss of Paradise,
Beyond all passion and strife and strain.
What fate removed you from earth's domain
And left me hapless and heartsick there?　　　　250
Since parting was set between us twain
I have been a joyless jeweler."

2

That jewel then with fair gems fraught
Lifted her face with eyes of grey,
Set on her crown and stood in thought,　　　　255
And soberly then I heard her say,
"Sir, your tale is told for nought,
To say your pearl has gone away
That is closed in a coffer so cunningly wrought
As this same garden green and gay,　　　　260
And here forever in joy to stay
Where lack nor loss can never come near;
Here were a casket fit to display
A prize for a proper jeweler.

3

"But, jeweler, if your mind is bound   265
To mourn for a gem in solitude,
Your care has set you a course unsound,
And a cause of a moment maddens your mood;
You lost a rose that grew in the ground:
A flower that fails and is not renewed,   270
But such is the coffer closing it round,
With the worth of a pearl it is now imbued.
And fate, you say, has robbed you of good,
That rendered you profit free and clear;
You blame a blessing misunderstood: 275
You are no proper jeweler."

4

A jewel to me then was this guest
And jewels her gentle sayings were.
"O blissful one," I said, "and best,
You have healed me wholly of heartache here!   280
To be excused I make request:
My pearl was away, I knew not where;
Now I have found it, now I shall rest,
And live with it ever, and make good cheer,
And love the Lord and his laws revere   285
That brought me the blissful sight of her.
Let me once cross and behold you near,
And I am a joyful jeweler!"

5

"Jeweler," said that gem at this,
"Such mockery comes of mortal pride!   290
Most ill-advised your answer is
And errors grave your thoughts misguide.
Three statements you have made amiss;
Your words from your wit have wandered wide;
You think me set in this vale of bliss   295
For so you see me, the brook beside;
The second, you say you shall abide
With me in this far country here;
The third, to cross this deep divide,
Behooves no joyful jeweler.   300

VI

1

"I hold that jeweler little to praise
Who believes no more than meets the eye,
And little courtesy he displays
Who doubts the word of the Lord on high
That faithfully pledged your flesh to raise   305
Though Fortune made it fail and die;
They twist the sense of his words and ways
Who believe what they see, and else deny;
And that is pride and obstinacy
And ill accords with honest intent,   310
To think each tale must be a lie
Except his reason give assent.

2

"Say, do you not, dissenting, strive
Against God's will that all should uphold?
Here in this land you mean to live—   315
You might ask leave to make so bold!
Nor can you with such ease contrive
To cross this water deep and cold;
Your body fair, with senses five,
Must first sink down in mire and mold,   320
For in Eden garden, in days of old,
Our fathers' father his life misspent;
Each man must suffer a death foretold
Ere God to this crossing give consent."

3

"Consent," said I, "to that hard fate   325
And you have cleft my heart in twain.
That which I lost I found but late—
And must I now forgo it again?
Why must I meet it and miss it straight?
My precious pearl has doubled my pain.   330
What use is treasure in worldly state
If a man must lose it and mourn in vain?
Now little I reck what trials remain,
What bitter exile and banishment,

For Fortune is bound to be my bane   335
And suffer I must by her consent."

4

"Such dire presentiments of distress,"
Said she, "I cannot comprehend;
But grief for a loss that matters less
Makes many miss what might amend.   340
Better to cross yourself, and bless
The name of the Lord, whatever he send;
No good can come of your willfulness;
Who bears bad luck must learn to bend.
Though like a stricken doe, my friend,   345
You plunge and bray, with loud lament,
This way and that, yet in the end
As he decrees, you must consent.

5

"Dissent, indict him through the years,
His step stirs not one inch astray.   350
No tittle is gained for all your tears,
Though you should grieve and never be gay.
Abate your bluster, be not so fierce,
And seek his grace as soon as you may,
For prayer has power to bite and pierce   355
And call compassion into play.
His mercy can wipe your tears away,
Redeem your loss, restore content,
But, grudge or be glad, agree or gainsay,
All lies with him to give consent."   360

VII

1

Then I assented, answering in dread,
"Let not my Lord be wrathful here
Though blindly I rave, with speech ill-sped;
Mourning had made me mad, or near.
As water flows from a fountainhead   365
I cast myself in his mercy clear;
Heap no reproaches on my head
Though I should stray, my dearest dear,

But speak in charity and good cheer;
Be merciful, remembering this: 370
You gave me a heavy grief to bear,
Who once were ground of all my bliss.

                            2

"My bliss you have been and bitterest woe;
The grief was the greater as time ran on;
Since last I looked for you high and low   375
I could not tell where my pearl had gone.
I rejoice in it now as long ago,
And when we parted we were as one;
God forbid I should vex you so—
We meet so seldom at any milestone.   380
Your courtesy is second to none;
I am of earth, and speak amiss,
But the mercy of Christ and Mary and John,
These are the ground of all my bliss.

                            3

"I see you set in bliss profound,   385
And I afflicted, felled by fate;
And little you care though I am bound
To suffer harm and hardship great;
But since we are met upon this ground
I would beseech, without debate,   390
That in sober speech you would expound
The life you lead both early and late.
Indeed, I am glad that your estate
Is raised to such honor and worthiness;
It is my joy to contemplate   395
And royal road of all my bliss."

                            4

"Now bliss befall you!" she replied
In form and feature that had no peer,
"And welcome here to walk and bide;
Such words are grateful to my ear.   400
Headstrong hearts and arrogant pride,
I tell you, are wholly detested here;
My Lord the Lamb is loath to chide,
For all are meek who behold him near.

And when in his house you shall appear,   405
Be wholly devout in humbleness,
For that delights my Lord so dear
That is the ground of all my bliss.

5

"A blissful life I lead, you say;
You ask in what station I reside;   410
You know when pearl first slipped away
I was tender of age, by time untried.
But my Lord the Lamb whom all obey,
He took me to him to be his bride,
Crowned me queen in bliss to stay,   415
Forever and ever glorified.
And seized of his heritage far and wide
Am I, his love, being wholly his;
His royal rank, his praise, his pride
Are root and ground of all my bliss."   420

VIII

1

"Oh, blissful one, can this be right?"
Said I, "Forgive me if I should err;
Are you the queen of heaven's height
Whom we in this world must all revere?
We believe in Mary, a virgin bright,   425
Who bore to man God's Son so dear;
Now who could assume her crown, by right,
But she in some feature fairer were?[4]
Yet as none is lovely like unto her,
We call her Phoenix of Araby,   430
Sent flawless from the artificer
As was our Queen of courtesy."

2

"Courteous Queen!" that blithe one said
Kneeling to ground with upturned face,
"Matchless Mother, most lovely Maid,   435
Blessed beginner of every grace!"
Then rose she up, and silent stayed,
And spoke to me across that space:

"Sir, gifts are gained here, and prizes paid,
But none on another presumes or preys.   440
Empress peerless ever to praise
Of heaven and earth and hell is she,
Yet puts no man from his rightful place,
For she is Queen of courtesy.

3

"The court of the kingdom whose crown I bear   445
Has a property by nature and name:
Each who gains admittance there
Is king of that realm, or queen of the same,
And none would lessen the others' share
But each one, glad of the others' fame,   450
Would wish their crowns five times as fair,
Had they the power of amending them;
But she who bore Jesu in Bethlehem
Over all of us here has sovereignty,
And none of our number carps at that claim,   455
For she is Queen of courtesy.

4

"By courtesy, so says St. Paul,°
We are members of Christ in joy profound,
As head, arms, legs, and navel and all
Are parts of one person hale and sound;   460
Likewise each Christian soul I call
A loyal limb of the Lord renowned;
Now what dispute could ever befall
Between two limbs in a body bound?
Though hand or wrist bear a golden round,   465
Your head will never the sorrier be:
Just so in love is each of us crowned
A king or queen by courtesy."

5

"Courtesy, no doubt, there is,
And charity rife your ranks among;   470
Yet truly—take it not amiss—

° 1 Corinthians 12.12–21, 26–27.

I cannot but think your words are wrong.
You set yourself too high in this,
To be crowned a queen, that was so young;
Why, what more honor might be his   475
That had lived in hardship late and long
And suffered pains and penance strong
To purchase bliss in heaven on high?
How might he more have thriven in throng
Than be crowned a king by courtesy?   480

IX

1

"That courtesy too free appears
If all be true as you portray;
You lived in our country not two years—
You could not please the Lord, or pray,
Or say 'Our Father,' or Creed rehearse—   485
And crowned a queen the very first day!
I cannot well believe my ears,
That God could go so far astray.
The style of countess, so I would say,
Were fair enough to attain unto,   490
Or a lesser rank in heaven's array,
But a queen! It is beyond your due."

2

"Beyond all due his bounty flows,"
So answered she in words benign;
"For all is justice that he does,   495
And truth is in his each design.
As the tale in the Gospel of Matthew goes
In the mass that blesses the bread and wine,
In parable his words propose
A likeness to the realm divine.°   500
A man possessed a vineyard fine—
So runs the tale in sermon true—
The time was come to tend the vine
By tasks assigned in order due.

° Matthew 20.1–16.

3

"The laborers duly gathered round;   505
The lord rose up by daybreak bright,
Sought at the market-place, and found
Some who would serve his turn aright.
By the same bargain each was bound:
Let a penny a day his pains requite;   510
Then forth they go into his ground
And prune and bind and put things right.
He went back late by morning light,
Found idle fellows not a few;
'Why stand you idle here in sight?   515
Has not this day its service due?'

4

" 'Duly we came ere break of day,'
So answered they in unison;
'The sun has risen and here we stay
And look for labor and yet find none.'   520
'Go to the vine; do what you may,'
So said the lord, 'till day is done;
Promptly at nightfall I shall pay
Such hire as each by right has won.'
So at the vine they labored on,   525
And still the lord, the long day through,
Brought in new workmen one by one
Till dusk approached at season due.

5

"When time was due of evensong,
The sunset but one hour away,   530
He saw there idle men in throng
And had these sober words to say:
'Why stand you idle all day long?'
None had required their help, said they.
'Go to the vine, young men and strong,   535
And do as much there as you may.'
Soon the earth grew dim and grey;
The sun long since had sunk from view;
He summoned them to take their pay;
The day had passed its limit due.   540

X

1

"Duly the lord, at day's decline,
Said to the steward, 'Sir, proceed;
Pay what I owe this folk of mine;
And lest men chide me here, take heed:
Set them all in a single line,[5]   545
Give each a penny as agreed;
Start with the last that came to the vine,
And let the first the last succeed.'
And then the first began to plead;
Long had they toiled, they said and swore;   550
'These in an hour had done their deed;
It seems to us we should have more.

2

" 'More have we served, who suffered through
The heat of the day till evening came,
Than these who stayed but an hour or two,   555
Yet you allow them equal claim.'
Then said the lord to one of that crew,
'Friend, I will not change the game;
Take your wage and away with you!
I offered a penny, to all the same;   560
Why begin to bicker and blame?
Was not our covenant set of yore?
Higher than covenant none should aim;
Why should you then ask for more?

3

" 'More, am I not at liberty   565
To give my own as I wish to do?
Or have you lifted an evil eye,
As I am good, to none untrue?'
'Thus,' says Christ, 'shall I shift it awry:
The last shall be the first in the queue,   570
And the first the last,[6] were he never so spry,
For many are called, but friends are few.'
So poor men take their portion too,
Though late they came and puny they were,

And though they make but little ado,   575
The mercy of God is much the more.

4

"More of ladyship here is mine,
Of life in flower and never to fade,
Than any man in the world could win
By right and right alone," she said.   580
"Although but late I began in the vine—
I came at evening, as Fortune bade—
The lord allowed me first in the line
And then and there I was fully paid.
There were others came early and later stayed,   585
Who labored long and sweated sore,
And still their payment is delayed,
Shall be, perhaps, for many years more."

5

Then with more discourse I demurred:
"There seems small reason in this narration: 590
God's justice carries across the board
Or Holy Writ is prevarication!
In the psalter of David there stands a word
Admits no cavil or disputation:°
'You render to each his just reward,   595
O ruler of every dispensation!'
Now he who all day kept his station,
If you to payment come in before,
Then the less, the more remuneration,
And ever alike, the less, the more."   600

XI

1

"Of more and less," she answered straight,
"In the Kingdom of God, no risk obtains,
For each is paid at the selfsame rate
No matter how little or great his gains.
No niggard is our chief of state,   605
Be it soft or harsh his will ordains;

° Psalm 61.12 (A.V. 62).

His gifts gush forth like a spring in spate
Or a stream in a gulley that runs in rains.
His portion is large whose prayers and pains
Please him who rescues when sinners call.   610
No bliss in heaven but he attains:
The grace of God is enough for all.

2

"Yet for all that, you stubbornly strive
To prove I have taken too great a fee;
You say I, the last to arrive,   615
Am not worthy so high degree.
When was there ever a man alive,
Were none so pious and pure as he,
Who by some transgression did not contrive
To forfeit the bliss of eternity?   620
And the older, the oftener the case must be
That he lapsed into sins both great and small.
Then mercy and grace must second his plea:
The grace of God is enough for all.

3

"But grace enough have the innocent: 625
When first they see the light of day
To the water of baptism they are sent
And brought to the vine without delay.
At once the light, its splendor spent,
Bows down to darkness and decay;   630
They had done no harm ere home they went;
From the Master's hands they take their pay.
Why should be not acknowledge them, pray?
They were there with the rest, they came at his call—
Yes, and give them their hire straightway: 635
The grace of God is enough for all.

4

"It is known well enough, the human race
Was formed to live in pure delight.
Our first forefather altered that case
By an apple of which he took a bite.   640
We all were damned by that disgrace
To die in sorrow and desperate plight

And then in hell to take our place
And dwell there lost in eternal night.°
But then there came a remedy right: 645
Rich blood ran down rood-tree tall
And with it flowed forth water bright:
The grace of God was enough for all.†

5

"Enough for all flowed from that well,
Blood and water plain to behold: 650
By the blood our souls were saved from hell
And the second death decreed of old.°°
The water is baptism, truth to tell,
That followed the spearhead keen and cold,
Old Adam's deadly guilt to dispel   655
That swamped us in sins a thousandfold.
Now all is withdrawn that ever could hold
Mankind from bliss, since Adam's fall,
And that was redeemed at a time foretold
And the grace of God is enough for all.   660

XII

1

"Grace enough that man can have
Who is penitent, having sinned anew,
If with sorrow at heart he cry and crave
And perform the penance that must ensue.
But by right reason, that cannot rave,   665
The innocent ever receives his due:
To punish the guiltless with the knave
Is a plan God never was party to.
The guilty, by contrition true,
Can attain to mercy requisite,   670
But he that never had guile in view,
The innocent is safe and right.

° Genesis 3.17–19; Matthew 13.41–42; Romans 5.12.
† John 19.34; Ephesians 1.3–7.
°° Revelation 20.14.

2

"I know right reason in this case
And thereto cite authority:
The righteous man shall see his face   675
And the innocent bear him company.
So in a verse the psalter says,*
'Lord, who shall climb your hill on high
Or rest within your holy place?'
And readily then he makes reply: 680
'Hands that did no injury,
Heart that was always pure and light:
There shall his steps be stayed in joy';
The innocent is safe by right.

3

"The righteous also in due time,   685
He shall approach that noble tor,
Who cozens his neighbor with no crime
Nor wastes his life in sin impure.
King Solomon tells in text sublime
Of Wisdom and her honored lore;†   690
By narrow ways she guided him
And lo! God's kingdom lay before.
As who should say, 'You distant shore—
Win it you may ere fall of night
If you make haste'; but evermore   695
The innocent is safe by right.

4

"Of the righteous man I find report
In the psalter of David, if ever you spied it:**
'Call not your servant, Lord, to court,
For judgment is grim if justice guide it.'   700
And when to that seat you must resort
Where each man's case shall be decided,
Claim the right, you may be caught short.
By this same proof I have provided.
But he who, scourged and sore derided,   705

* Psalm 23.3–4 (A.V. 24).
† Wisdom 10.9–10 (A.V. classified as Apocryphal).
** Psalm 142.2 (A.V. 143).

Bled on the cross through mortal spite,
Grant that your sentence be decided
By innocence and not by right.

5

"Who reads the Book of rightful fame
May learn of it infallibly   710
How good folk with their children came
To Jesus walking in Galilee.°
The touch of his hand they sought for them
For the goodness in him plain to see;
The disciples banned that deed with blame   715
And bade the children let him be.
But Jesus gathered them round his knee
And of that reprimand made light;
'Of such is the kingdom of heaven,' said he;
The innocent is safe by right.   720

XIII

1

"Jesus on his faithful smiled
And said, 'God's kingdom shall be won
By him who seeks it as a child,
For other entry-right is none.'
Harmless, steadfast, undefiled,   725
Unsullied bright to gaze upon,
When such stand knocking, meek and mild,
Straightway the gate shall be undone.
There is the endless bliss begun
That the jeweler sought in earthly estate   730
And sold all his goods, both woven and spun,
To purchase a pearl immaculate.†

2

"This immaculate pearl I tell you of,
The jeweler gave his wealth to gain,
Is like the realm of heaven above;   735
The Father of all things said it plain.
No spot it bears, nor blemish rough,

° Mark 10.13–16; Luke 18.15–17.
† Matthew 13.45–46.

But blithe in rondure ever to reign,[7]
And of righteousness it is prize and proof:
Lo, here on my breast it long has lain,   740
Bestowed by the Lamb so cruelly slain,
His peace to betoken and designate;
I bid you turn from the world insane
And purchase your pearl immaculate."

3

"Immaculate pearl whom white pearls crown,   745
Who bear," said I, "the pearl of price,
Who fashioned your form? Who made your gown?
Oh, he that wrought it was most wise!
Such beauty in nature never was known;
Pygmalion never painted your eyes,   750
Nor Aristotle, of long renown,
Discoursed of these wondrous properties,
Your gracious aspect, your angel guise,
More white than the lily, and delicate:
What duties high, what dignities   755
Are marked by the pearl immaculate?"

4

"My immaculate Lamb, my destiny sweet,"
Said she, "who can all harm repair,
He made me his mate in marriage meet,
Though once such a match unfitting were.   760
When I left your world of rain and sleet
He called me in joy to join him there:
'Come hither, my dove without deceit,
For you are spotless, past compare.°
He gave me strength, he made me fair,   765
He crowned me a virgin consecrate,
And washed in his blood these robes I wear,†
And clad me in pearls immaculate."

5

"Immaculate being, bright as flame,
In royalties set and sanctified,   770
Tell me now, what is that Lamb

° Canticle of Canticles 4.7, 5.2 (A.V. Song of Solomon).
† Apocalypse 7.13–14 (A.V. Revelation).

That sought you out to become his bride?
Over all others you pressed your claim
To live in honor with him allied,
Yet many a noble and worthy dame   775
For Christ's dear sake has suffered and died;
And you have thrust those others aside
And reserved for yourself that nuptial state,
Yourself all alone, so big with pride,
A matchless maid and immaculate?"   780

XIV

1

"Immaculate," came her answer clear,
"Unblemished am I, my peers among;
So much I claim with honor here,
But matchless—there you have it wrong.
We all are brides of the Lamb so dear,   785
One hundred and forty-four thousand strong,
In Apocalypse the words appear
As John beheld it and told with tongue.°
Thousands on thousands, virgins young,
He saw on Mount Sion in sacred dream,   790
Arrayed for the wedding in comely throng
In the city called New Jerusalem.

2[8]

"Of Jerusalem I speak perforce,
To tell his nature and degree,
My jewel dear, my joy's sole source,   795
My Lamb, my lord, my love, all three.
In the prophet Isaiah we find discourse
Of him and his humility,†
Condemned and martyred without remorse
And on false charges of felony,   800
As a sheep to the slaughter led was he,
As a lamb to the shearers meek and tame;
His lips were sealed to all inquiry
When Jews were his judge in Jerusalem.

° Apocalypse 14.1 (A.V. Revelation).
† Isaiah 53.7, 9.

3

"In Jerusalem my true love died,   805
Rent by rude hands with pain and woe;
Freely he perished for our pride,
And suffered our doom in mortal throe.°
His blessèd face, or ever he died,
Was made to bleed by many a blow;†   810
For sin he set his power aside
Though never he sinned who suffered so.
For us he was beaten and bowed low
And racked on the rood-tree rough and grim,
And meek as the lamb with fleece of snow   815
He breathed his last in Jerusalem.

4

"In Jerusalem, Jordan, and Galilee,
When John the Baptist preached abroad,
The words with Isaiah well agree
That he said when Jesus before him stood;°°   820
He made of him this prophecy:
'Steadfast as stone, O Lamb of God,
Who takes away the iniquity
That all this world has wrought in blood';
And he was guiltless and ever good,   825
Yet bore our sins and atoned for them;
O who can reckon his parenthood
Who perished for us in Jerusalem?

5

"In Jerusalem my lover true
Appeared as a lamb of purest white   830
In the eyes of the prophets old and new
For his meck mien and piteous plight.
The third fits well with the other two,
In Revelation written aright;††
Where the saints sat round in retinue   835
The Apostle saw him throned in light,
Bearing the book with pages bright

° Isaiah 53.4–5.
† Matthew 26.67.
°° John 1.29.
†† Apocalypse 5.1, 6–7 (A.V. Revelation).

And the seven seals set round the rim,
And all hosts trembled at that sight,
In hell, in earth, and Jerusalem.   840

XV

1

"This Jerusalem Lamb in his array
Was whiter far than tongue could tell;
No spot or speck might on him stay,
His fair rich fleece did so excel.
And so each sinless soul, I say,   845
Is a worthy wife with the Lamb to dwell,
And though he fetch a score each day
No strife is stirred in our citadel,
But would each brought four others as well—
The more the merrier in blessedness!   850
Our love is increased as our numbers swell,
And honor more and never the less.

2

"Less of bliss none brings us here
Who bear the pearl upon our breast;
No mark of strife could ever appear   855
Where the precious pearl is worn for crest.
Our bodies lie on earthen bier,
And you go grieving, sore distressed,
But we, with knowledge full and clear,
See in one death all wrong redressed.   860
The Lamb has laid our cares to rest;
We partake of his table in joyfulness;
Each one's share of bliss is best,
Nor ever in honor any the less.

3

"Lest less you believe, incline your ear   865
To the Book of Revelation true:*
'I saw,' says John, 'the Lamb appear
On the Mount of Sion, all white of hue,
With a hundred thousand maidens dear

---

* Apocalypse 14.1–5 (A.V. Revelation).

And forty-four thousand more in view;   870
On all their foreheads written were
The name of the Lamb, of his Father too.
But then in heaven a clamor grew,
Like waters running in rapid race;
As thunder crashes in storm-cloud blue,   875
Such was that sound, and nothing less.

4

" 'Nevertheless, though it shouted shrill
And made the heavens resound again,
I heard them sing upon that hill
A new song, a most noble strain;   880
As harpers touch their harps with skill
Their voices lifted, full and plain;
And well they followed with a will
The phrases of that fair refrain.
Before his throne who ever shall reign   885
And the four beasts ranged about the dais°
And the solemn elders of that domain,†
Great was their song, and grew no less.

5

" 'Nevertheless, there was none had might
Or for all his art might ever aspire   890
To sing that song, save those in white
Who follow the Lamb their lord and sire;
For they are redeemed from earth's dark night
As first fruits given to God entire,
And joined with the Lamb on Sion's height,   895
As like himself in speech and attire,
For never, in deed or heart's desire,
Their tongues were touched with untruthfulness;
And none can sever that sinless choir
From that master immaculate, nevertheless.' "   900

6

"Never less welcome let me find,"
Said I, "for the queries I propose;
I should not tempt your noble mind

° Apocalypse 4.6–7 (A.V. Revelation).
† Apocalypse 4.4 (A.V. Revelation).

Whom Christ the Lord to his chamber chose.
I am of mire and mere mankind,   905
And you so rich and rare a rose,
And here to eternal bliss assigned
Where joy fails not, but forever grows.
Now, dame, whom simplicity's self endows,
I would beseech a favor express,   910
And though I am rough and rude, God knows,
Let it be granted nevertheless.

XVI

1

"Nevertheless, if you can see
In my request a reason sound,
Deny not my dejected plea,   915
But where grace is, let grace abound.
Have you no hall, no hostelry,
To dwell in and meet in daily round?
You tell of Jerusalem rich and free
Where reigned King David the renowned,   920
But that cannot be near this ground
But lies in Judea, by reckoning right;
As you under moon are flawless found,
Your lodgings should be wholly bright.

2

"These holy virgins in radiant guise,   925
By thousands thronged in processional—
That city must be of uncommon size
That keeps you together, one and all.
It were not fit such jewels of price
Should lie unsheltered by roof or wall,   930
Yet where these river-banks arise
I see no building large or small.
Beside this stream celestial
You linger alone, none else in sight;
If you have another house or hall,   935
Show me that dwelling wholly bright."

3

That wholly blissful, that spice heaven-sent,
Declared, "In Judea's fair demesne
The city lies, where the Lamb once went
To suffer for man death's anguish keen.   940
The old Jerusalem by that is meant,
For there the old guilt was canceled clean,
But the new, in vision prescient,
John saw sent down from God pristine.*
The spotless Lamb of gracious mien   945
Has carried us all to that fair site,
And as in his flock no fleck is seen,
His hallowed halls are wholly bright.

4

"Two holy cities I figure forth;
One name suits well with both of these,   950
Which in the language of your birth
Is 'City of God,' or 'Sight of Peace.'†
In the one the Lamb brought peace on earth
Who suffered for our iniquities;
In the other is peace with heavenly mirth,   955
And ever to last, and never to cease.
And to that city in glad release
From fleshly decay our souls take flight;
There glory and bliss shall ever increase
In the household that is wholly bright."   960

5

"Holy maid compassionate,"
Said I to that fresh flower and gay,
"Let me approach those ramparts great
And see the chamber where you stay."
"The Lord forbids," she answered straight,   965
"That a stranger in his streets should stray,
But through the Lamb enthroned in state
I have won you a sight of it this day.
Behold it from far off you may,
But no man's foot may there alight;   970

---

* Apocalypse 21.2 (A.V. Revelation).
† Apocalypse 3.12 (A.V. Revelation); Ezekiel 13.16.

You have no power to walk that way
Save as a spirit wholly bright.

XVII

1

"This holy city that I may show,
Walk upwards toward the river's head,
And here against you I shall go   975
Until to a hill your path has led."
Then to stir I was not slow,
But under leafy boughs I sped
Until from a hill I looked below
And saw the city, as she had said,   980
Beyond the stream in splendor spread,
That brighter than shafts of sunlight shone.
In Apocalypse it may all be read
As he set it forth, the apostle John.°

2

As John the apostle saw it of old   985
I saw the city beyond the stream,
Jerusalem the new and fair to behold,
Sent down from heaven by power supreme.
The streets were paved with precious gold,
As flawless pure as glass agleam,   990
Based on bright gems of worth untold,
Foundation-stones twelvefold in team;
And set in series without a seam,
Each level was a single stone,
As he beheld it in sacred dream   995
In Apocalypse, the apostle John.

3

As John had named them in writ divine
Each stone in order by name I knew;
Jasper was the first in line;
At the lowest level it came in view;   1000
Green ingrained I saw it shine.
The second was the sapphire blue;

° Apocalypse 21.10–27, 22.1–2 (A.V. Revelation).

The clear chalcedony, rare and fine,
Was third in degree in order due.
The fourth the emerald green of hue;   1005
Sardonyx fifth was set thereon;
The sixth the ruby he saw ensue
In Apocalypse, the apostle John.

4

To these John joined the chrysolite,
The seventh in that foundation's face;   1010
The eighth the beryl clear and white,
The twin-hued topaz ninth to trace;
The chrysoprase tenth in order right;
Jacinth held the eleventh place;
The twelfth, the amethyst most of might,   1015
Blent blue and purple in royal blaze.
The jasper walls above that base
Like lustrous glass to gaze upon;
I knew them all by his every phrase
In Apocalypse, the apostle John.   1020

5

As John had written, so I was ware
How broad and steep was each great tier;
As long as broad as high foursquare
The city towered on twelvefold pier.
The streets like glass in brilliance bare,   1025
The walls like sheen on parchment sheer;
The dwellings all with gemstones rare
Arrayed in radiance far and near.
The sides of that perimeter
Twelve thousand furlongs spanned, each one;   1030
Length, breadth, and height were measured there
Before his eyes, the apostle John.

XVIII

1

Yet more, John saw on every side
Three gateways set commensurate,
So twelve I counted in compass wide,   1035
The portals rich with precious plate.

Each gate a pearl of princely pride,
Unfading, past all earthly fate,
On which a name was signified
Of Israel's sons, in order of date,   1040
That is, by birthright ranked in state,
The eldest ever the foremost one.
The streets were alight both early and late;
They needed neither sun nor moon.

2

Sun and moon were far surpassed;   1045
The Lord was their lamp eternally,
The Lamb their lantern ever to last
Made bright that seat of sovereignty.
Through roof and wall my looking passed,
Pure substance hindered not to see;   1050
There I beheld the throne steadfast
With the emblems that about it be,
As John in text gave testimony;
Upon it sat the Lord triune;
A river therefrom ran fresh and free,[9]   1055
More bright by far than sun or moon.

3

Sun nor moon shone never so fair
As that flood of plenteous waters pure;
Full it flowed in each thoroughfare;
No filth or taint its brightness bore.   1060
Church they had none, nor chapel there,
House of worship, nor need therefor;
The Almighty was their place of prayer,
The Lamb the sacrifice all to restore.
No lock was set on gate or door   1065
But evermore open both night and noon;
None may take refuge on that floor
Who bears any spot beneath the moon.[10]

4

The moon has in that reign no right;
Too spotty she is, of body austere;   1070
And they who dwell there know no night—
Of what avail her varying sphere?

And set beside that wondrous light
That shines upon the waters clear
The planets would lose their lustre quite,   1075
And the sun itself would pale appear.
Beside the river are trees that bear
Twelve fruits of life their boughs upon;
Twelve times a year they burgeon there
And renew themselves with every moon.   1080

5

Beneath the moon so much amazed
No fleshly heart could bear to be
As by that city on which I gazed,
Its form so wondrous was to see.
As a quail that couches, dumb and dazed,   1085
I stared on that great symmetry;
Nor rest nor travail my soul could taste,
Pure radiance so had ravished me.
For this I say with certainty:
Had a man in the body borne that boon,   1090
No doctor's art, for fame or fee,
Had saved his life beneath the moon.

XIX

1

As the great moon begins to shine
While lingers still the light of day,[11]
So in those ramparts crystalline   1095
I saw a procession wend its way.
Without a summons, without a sign,
The city was full in vast array
Of maidens in such raiment fine
As my blissful one had worn that day.   1100
As she was crowned, so crowned were they;
Adorned with pearls, in garments white;
And in like fashion, gleaming gay,
They bore the pearl of great delight.

2

With great delight, serene and slow,   1105
They moved through every golden street;

Thousands on thousands, row on row,
All in one raiment shining sweet.
Who gladdest looked, was hard to know;
The Lamb led on at station meet,   1110
Seven horns of gold upon his brow,°
His robe like pearls with rays replete.
Soon they approached God's mighty seat;
Though thick in throng, unhurried quite;
As maidens at communion meet   1115
They moved along with great delight.

                        3

Delight that at his coming grew
Was greater than my tongue can tell;
The elders when he came in view
Prostrate as one before him fell;   1120
Hosts of angels in retinue
Cast incense forth of sweetest smell;
Then all in concert praised anew
That jewel with whom in joy they dwell.†
The sound could pierce through the earth to hell   1125
When the powers of heaven in song unite;
To share his praises in citadel
My heart indeed had great delight.

                        4

Delight and wonder filled me in flood
To hear all heaven the Lamb acclaim;   1130
Gladdest he was, most kind and good
Of any that ever was known to fame.
His dress so white, so mild his mood,
His looks so gracious, himself the same;
But a wound there was, and wide it stood,   1135
Thrust near his heart with deadly aim.
Down his white side the red blood came;
"O God," thought I, "who had such spite?
A breast should consume with sorrow and shame
Ere in such deeds it took delight."   1140

° Apocalypse 5.6 (A.V. Revelation).
† Apocalypse 5.8, 11–14 (A.V. Revelation).

5

The Lamb's delight was clearly seen,
Though a bitter wound he had to bear;
So glorious was his gaze serene,
It gladdened all who beheld him there.
I looked where that bright host had been, 1145
How charged with life, how changed they were.
And then I saw my little queen
That I thought but now I had stood so near.
Lord! how she laughed and made good cheer
Among her friends, who was so white! 1150
To rush in the river then and there
I longed with love and great delight.

XX

1

Moved by delight of sight and sound,
My maddened mind all fate defied.
I would follow her there, my newly found, 1155
Beyond the river though she must bide.
I thought that nothing could turn me round,
Forestall me, or stop me in mid-stride,
And wade I would from the nearer ground
And breast the stream, though I sank and died. 1160
But soon those thoughts were thrust aside;
As I made for the river incontinent
I was summoned away and my wish denied:
My Prince therewith was not content.

2

It contented him not that I, distraught, 1165
Should dare the river that rimmed the glade;
Though reckless I was, and overwrought,
In a moment's space my steps were stayed.
For just as I started from the spot
I was reft of my dream and left dismayed; 1170
I waked in that same garden-plot,[12]
On that same mound my head was laid.
I stretched my hand where Pearl had strayed;
Great fear befell me, and wonderment;

And, sighing, to myself I said,   1175
"Let all things be to his content."

3

I was ill content to be dispossessed
Of the sight of her that had no peer
Amid those scenes so bright and blessed;
Such longing seized me, I swooned, or near;   1180
Then sorrow broke from my burning breast;
"O honored Pearl," I said, "how dear
Was your every word and wise behest
In this true vision vouchsafed me here.
If you in a garland never sere   1185
Are set by that Prince all-provident,
Then happy am I in dungeon drear
That he with you is well content."

4

Had I but sought to content my Lord
And taken his gifts without regret,   1190
And held my place and heeded the word
Of the noble Pearl so strangely met,
Drawn heavenward by divine accord
I had seen and heard more mysteries yet;
But always men would have and hoard   1195
And gain the more, the more they get.
So banished I was, by cares beset,
From realms eternal untimely sent;
How madly, Lord, they strive and fret
Whose acts accord not with your content!   1200

5

To content that Prince and well agree,
Good Christians can with ease incline,
For day and night he has proved to be
A Lord, a God, a friend benign.
These words came over the mound to me   1205
As I mourned my Pearl so flawless fine,
And to God committed her full and free,
With Christ's dear blessing bestowing mine,
As in the form of bread and wine
Is shown us daily in sacrament;   1210

O may we serve him well, and shine
As precious pearls to his content.

Amen.

Notes: *Pearl*

1. I.1.9: **In a garden of herbs I lost my dear.** We infer that the garden is enclosed, because the speaker says he entered it (I.4.1); later, as the dreamer, he sees the pearl-maiden standing in what she calls a garden (V.2.8); it too is "enclosed," barred from him by the river he cannot cross (V.5.11–12). Space in the vision is symbolic rather than realistic: the garden beyond the river is also the heavenly Jerusalem, the walled city to which the maiden says the Lamb has transported her (XVI.3.9–10) and in which the dreamer sees her in the procession in section XIX. Garden and city are interchangeable symbols for the kingdom of heaven; each serves to make some aspect of it more accessible to the human imagination. The garden the speaker enters in section I is said to contain both herbs (1.9) and spices (3.1). The two are not wholly distinct; plants of both classes have medicinal and preservative powers. The former prefigure the healing of the dreamer's sorrow in the course of his dream; the latter, the blissful immortality of the pearl-maiden, which, as a faithful Christian, the dreamer can hope to attain himself. Spices in particular have a fragrance symbolically associated with the divine realm and all things pertaining to it; they appear frequently in the imagery of the Old Testament Canticle of Canticles, or Song of Songs, which was interpreted as an allegory signifying the love of Christ for the Church. It is presumably the fragrance of the spices in the garden that lulls the speaker to sleep (I.5.10–12). The speaker refers to the maiden as a "spice" in section XVI (3.1); in the original poem, but not in my translation, he also refers to her thus in section IV (5.7). The poet is probably punning here on two words in Middle English; each was derived ultimately from Latin *species*, and each could be spelled either *spice* or *spece*. One was equivalent in meaning to modern *spice*, the other meant "a visible shape, appearance or semblance." Both meanings apply to the maiden.
2. II.4.11: **I came to the shore of a waterway.** As the dreamer will learn, the "shore" of the river at which he has arrived marks the closed boundary of the landscape within which, up to now, he has moved freely. Late in the poem, the dreamer is instructed by the pearl-maiden to follow the stream uphill toward its "head" (XVII.1.2); when he has done so, he sees the heavenly Jerusalem and within it a river that runs from the throne of God (XVIII.2.11–12). This is the "river of water of life" referred to in Apocalypse (Revelation) 22.1; it does not flow in a single direction but radiates outward in all directions, filling "each thoroughfare" (XVIII.3.3) of the city. The stream that both brings the dreamer and his Pearl together and separates them would seem to be continuous with it.
3. III.2.5–6: **It could not be but Paradise Lay beyond those blissful banks, thought I.** It is not clear whether the speaker is mistakenly thinking of the "earthly Paradise," believed to be the still existent, though unknown, site of the Garden of Eden, or the "celestial Paradise," i.e., the heavenly realm. It is the latter that lies beyond the banks, on the river's farther side.

4. VIII.1.7–8: **Now who could assume her crown, by right, But she in some feature fairer were?** These lines express one part of an important thematic opposition in the poem that I have touched on in the "Introduction" (p. 116); it comes to the foreground in the parable of the vineyard in section IX. The opposed concepts might be called "comparative value" and "absolute value," or "that which is measurable" and "that which transcends measurement." See the note to X.1.5.

5. X.1.5: **Set them all in a single line.** The line (called a *rawe* or "row" in the original) is by definition "linear" or sequential, visibly so as time is invisibly so. Both lines and units of time can be measured; they have "first" and "last" points and are divisible into inches or minutes. The workers that arrived first at the vine plead that positions in the line should also correspond to a measured series of payments or values, from smallest to largest, corresponding to a range between shortest and longest periods of time.

6. X.3.6: **The last shall be the first in the queue, and the first the last.** This statement in the parable was interpreted by the church fathers as having two different meanings: that the first and last positions are to be reversed, and that they are to be made equal. The two interpretations embody the complementarity between "comparative" and "absolute"—in spatial terms, between positions in a line and positions on the circumference of a circle. As the line of workers is the major symbol of linearity in the poem, the major symbol of circularity is the pearl.

7. XIII.2.5: **No spot it bears, nor blemish rough, But blithe in rondure ever to reign.** As the immaculate brightness of the pearl betokens the freedom from sin that merits eternal life, so its rondure or circularity betokens eternity itself.

8. XIV.2–3, 4, 5: The envisagement of Christ the redeemer as a sacrificial lamb in this section proceeds in three stages of increasing profundity. In the first, it has the form of a simile: Jesus, in his silence at the time of his condemnation, is *like* a lamb. In the second, it is stated as a metaphor: John the Baptist addresses Jesus as "Lamb of God." In the third, the form of a lamb appears as a symbolic personification of Christ in heaven, part of the supernatural vision described by St. John in the Apocalypse.

9. XVIII.2.11: **A river therefrom ran fresh and free.** See the note to II.4.11.

10. XVIII.3.11–12: **None may take refuge on that floor Who bears any spot beneath the moon.** We spend our lives on earth "beneath the moon," dominated by changes of fortune and state that resemble the moon's waxing and waning. This "sublunary" realm of time is contrasted by the poet with the "translunary" realm of eternity where there is no need of moonlight or sunlight. We learn from stanza 5 that the speaker, translated out of the mortal body, has left the sublunary realm behind him. Had he remained there, the shock of the vision of the celestial Jerusalem would have taken his life.

11. XIX.1.1–2: **As the great moon begins to shine While lingers still the light of day.** Here the image of the risen full moon is transitional between mortal and eternal realms. The dreamer, looking toward it from earth, seems to see the life of the celestial city within its circle, and the city itself, having been imagined as a cube in XVII.5, is now imagined as circular. The throne of God is at its center, and every street is a radius leading toward it in a kind of hyperspace, filled simultaneously by the river of life and the members of the procession.

12. XX.2.7: **I waked in that same garden plot.** The poet makes it clear that the speaker wakens exactly where he had fallen asleep, on the ground where his pearl

lies buried. On awakening, he stretches out his hand, as he had stretched it out in the earlier scene (I.I.5.2). This correspondence between the beginning and end of the dream and the verbal correspondence between the first line of the poem and the last work together to give the poem a kind of circularity of form, as a necklace changes from a line to a circle when its two ends are linked.

Biblical Sources

1. Apocalypse 5.6, 8, 11–14

6. And I saw: and behold in the midst of the throne and of the four living creatures, and in the midst of the ancients, a Lamb standing as it were slain, having seven horns and seven eyes. . . .

8. And . . . the four living creatures, and the four and twenty ancients fell down before the Lamb, having every one of them harps, and golden vials full of odours. . . .

11. And I beheld, and I heard the voice of many angels round about the throne, and the living creatures, and the ancients; and the number of them was thousands of thousands,

12. Saying with a loud voice: The Lamb that was slain is worthy to receive power, and divinity, and wisdom, and strength, and honour, and glory, and benediction.

13. And every creature, which is in heaven, and on the earth, and under the earth, and such as are in the sea, and all that are in them: I heard all saying: to him that sitteth on the throne, and to the Lamb, benediction, and honour, and glory, and power, for ever and ever.

14. And the four living creatures said: Amen. And the four and twenty ancients fell down on their faces, and adored him that liveth for ever and ever.

2. Apocalypse 14.1–5

1. And I beheld, and lo a lamb stood upon mount Sion, and with him an hundred forty-four thousand, having his name, and the name of his Father, written on their foreheads.

2. And I heard a voice from heaven, as the noise of many waters, and as the voice of great thunder; and the voice which I heard, was as the voice of harpers, harping on their harps.

3. And they sung as it were a new canticle, before the throne, and before the four living creatures, and the ancients; and no man could say the canticle,

but those hundred forty-four thousand, who were purchased from the earth.

4. These are they who were not defiled with women, for they are virgins. These follow the Lamb whithersoever he goeth. These were purchased from among men, the firstfruits to God and to the Lamb:

5. And in their mouth there was found no lie; for they are without spot before the throne of God.

3. Apocalypse 21.10–27

10. And he took me up in spirit to a great and high mountain: and he shewed me the holy city Jerusalem coming down out of heaven from God,

11. Having the glory of God, and the light thereof was like to a precious stone, as to the jasper stone, even as crystal.

12. And it had a wall great and high, having twelve gates, and in the gates twelve angels, and names written thereon, which are the names of the twelve tribes of the children of Israel.

13. On the east, three gates: and on the north, three gates: and on the south, three gates: and on the west, three gates.

14. And the wall of the city had twelve foundations, and in them, the twelve names of the twelve apostles of the Lamb.

15. And he that spoke with me, had a measure of a reed of gold, to measure the city and the gates thereof, and the wall.

16. And the city lieth in a foursquare, and the length thereof is as great as the breadth: and he measured the city with the golden reed for twelve thousand furlongs, and the length and the height and the breadth thereof are equal.

17. And he measured the wall thereof an hundred forty-four cubits, the measure of a man, which is of the angel.

18. And the building of the wall thereof was of jasper stone: but the city itself pure gold, like to clear glass.

19. And the foundations of the wall of the city were adorned with all manner of precious stones. The first foundation was jasper: the second, sapphire: the third, a chalcedony: the fourth, an emerald:

20. The fifth sardonyx: the sixth, sardius: the seventh, chrysolite: the eighth, beryl: the ninth, a topaz: the tenth, a chrysoprasus: the eleventh, a jacinth: the twelfth, an amethyst.

21. And the twelve gates are twelve pearls, one to each: and every several gate was of one several pearl. And the street of the city was pure gold, as it were transparent glass.

22. And I saw no temple therein. For the Lord God Almighty is the temple thereof, and the Lamb.

23. And the city hath no need of the sun, nor of the moon, to shine in it. For the glory of God hath enlightened it, and the Lamb is the lamp thereof.

24. And the nations shall walk in the light of it: and the kings of the earth shall bring their glory and honour into it.

25. And the gates thereof shall not be shut by day: for there shall be no night there.

26. And they shall bring the glory and honour of the nations into it.

27. There shall not enter into it any thing defiled, or that worketh abomination or maketh a lie, but they that are written in the book of the Lamb.

4. Apocalypse 22.1–2

1. And he showed me a river of water of life, clear as crystal, and proceeding from the throne of God and of the Lamb.

2. In the midst of the street thereof, and on both sides of the river, was the tree of life, bearing twelve fruits, yielding its fruits every month, and the leaves of the tree were for the healing of the nations.

The Metrical Forms

We cannot understand fully the metrical patterns of the *Gawain*-poet's verse unless we know something about how the English language was pronounced in the late fourteenth century in the northwest midland dialect area where he lived. A feature of crucial importance in this connection is the syllabic "final -*e*" that is often sounded between the stressed syllables of Chaucer's iambic verse, and always, where the word in question contains it, at the end of the line. In Chaucer's London English, this -*e* was probably pronounced in speech as well as in verse, at least in words pronounced with some degree of emphasis. It is my contention that in the spoken language of the *Gawain*-poet -*e* had wholly died out, though it continued to be reproduced in spelling (as it still is in modern words with "long vowels" like *came*, *hope*).[1] Accordingly, I believe that the alliterating lines of *Gawain* and *Patience* were read in the original with no sounding of -*e* within the line. Noun-adjective phrases preceded by the definite article, like "the good knight" and "the good man," which would have had four syllables in Chaucer's verse ("the goodë knight," "the goodë man") would have had three in the *Gawain*-poet's verse, as they do today, whether or not an *e* was appended to the adjective by the scribe who copied the manuscript. (In the manuscript original, we find "the gode knyght" in line 482, but "the god mon" in line 1179.) I concede the possibility that at the end of the alliterating line, -*e* was sounded where present —for example, in *Troyë* at the end of line 1. Such an archaizing mode of recitation would have been handed down from earlier times, along with the formulaic phrases that were part of the inherited tradition (see the "Introduction" to *Sir Gawain*, p. 3). I discuss below the more conservative, or Chaucer-like, treatment of -*e* in the rhymed lines of *Gawain* and *Pearl*.

If final -*e* is silent within the long alliterating line, it follows that modern translations can reproduce, and not merely approximate, the metrical patterns of the original, as I believe I have done. My line "There was meat, there was mirth, there was much joy" (*Gawain* 1007), for example, has exactly the same wording as the line in the original poem, and the same metrical pattern, except for the above-mentioned possibility of a sounded final -*e* in *joy* (Chaucer's *joyë*). In Chaucer's verse, *meat* and *mirth*, as well as *joy*,

---

1. I present these views at length in "The Phonological Evidence" and "The Metrical Evidence" in my *Sir Gawain and the Green Knight: A Stylistic and Metrical Study* (New Haven: Yale University Press, 1962).

had an -*e* that was sounded when not elided before a vowel. Because the patterns of the original are reproduced in my own verse, I see no reason to quote the Middle English version in illustrating them.

Alliterative verse as composed in the *Gawain*-poet's time had descended, with modifications reflecting changes in the language itself, from alliterative verse in Old English, which in turn was a Germanic inheritance. The tradition retained its vitality in the midland and northern regions of England in the second half of the fourteenth century but had fallen into disuse by the end of the fifteenth. Chaucer knew of it but did not compose in it himself. His Parson, in the prologue to the last of the *Canterbury Tales*, says "I am a southren man; I can nat geste [compose poetry] rum, ram, ruf, bi lettre."

Chaucer wrote exclusively in the rhymed verse that became predominant in English after the Norman Conquest, having developed in Europe in Latin and Old French. The ten-syllable iambic pentameter line in which most of the *Canterbury Tales* were written continued in use in English poetic tradition into the modern period, again with changes reflecting changes in the language. But the rhymed verse of *Sir Gawain* and *Pearl* is not iambic; it is more variable in syllable count than that written by Chaucer and his successor poets.

The *Gawain*-poet composed *Patience* entirely in alliterative verse, *Pearl* entirely in rhymed verse, and *Sir Gawain and the Green Knight* in a mixture of the two.

Alliterative Verse

The Basic Form

The so-called alliterative long line, as we find it in the works of the *Gawain*-poet, is best described in terms of a basic form that serves as a point of departure for a number of variations. The fact that this same basic form and these same variations appear in *Patience, Sir Gawain*, and *Purity* is one kind of evidence for the common authorship of the poems.

The rhythm of the lines that recurrently exemplify the basic form is easy to sense, as is the formal relationship between alliteration and stress. The line is divided into two half-lines; this division, called the caesura, is marked by a syntactic break of at least minor importance. Each half-line contains two stressed syllables, or, as I call them, chief syllables, for a total of four per line. Chief syllables are spaced temporally as the downbeats of successive measures are spaced in a musical piece played freely rather than metronomically. That is, we perceive them as recurring in a time continuum at regular, though not at exactly equal, intervals. The line can thus be described as having four "measures," in the musical sense of that word. Alliteration is not ornamental, as it is in most of the verse modern readers are familiar with, but a requirement of the form: the two chief syllables in most first half-lines alliterate with each other and with the first chief syllable of the second, for a total three alliterating syllables per line. There must be at least one alliterative link between half-lines. The chief syllable at the end of the line normally does not alliterate.

Some examples should make all this clearer. (I mark the vowels of stressed, or chief, syllables with a capital *C* above the line, and the first letters of stressed alliterating words with lower-case *a* below the line. The first letters of stressed nonalliterating syllables are marked *x*. The caesura in mid-line is marked /.) In the first pair of examples only, I indicate with vertical bars the "downbeats" that are heard, with slight variations of tempo, in freely played music.

```
                   C           C        C          C
     With all the |meat and the |mirth that |men could de|vise,
                   a           a   /   a              x


          C           C   C        C
     Such |gaiety and |glee, |glorious to |hear.
          a           a  /a        x
```

(Gawain 45–46)

```
            C           C        C          C
     But since a |plight called |Poverty is ap|pointed me |here,
                a           a        a          x


         C           C        C          C
     I shall |pair her with |Patience and |play along with |both.
         a           a   /    a              x
```

(Patience 35–36)

As the above examples show, chief syllables may be separated by one, two, or three "intermediate" syllables, most frequently by one or two. It is natural to read measures containing two and three intermediate syllables more rapidly than those containing only one.

Occasionally, chief syllables are juxtaposed, usually in the second half-line:

```
         C           C        C     C
     All the onlookers eyed him and edged nearer
         a           a   /    a     x
```

(Gawain 237)

In the above example, as is permissible, several different vowels alliterate with one another.

```
    C                 C              C   C
Buried within the bowels of the black earth
    a                 a     /        a   x
```
(*Patience* 363)

Note that in the above line the first two chief syllables are separated by four intermediate syllables.

Occasionally, the first half-line contains only one alliterating chief syllable:

```
        C        C         C            C
The stranger before him stood there erect.
        a        x        /a            x
```
(*Gawain* 332)

```
        C        C        C    C
To our merciful God, as Moses taught
        a        x   /    a    x
```
(*Patience* 238)

Sometimes the line contains two different alliterating letters; I mark these *a* and *b*. The pattern may be either *ab/ba* or *ab/ab*:

```
            C          C              C           C
And with undaunted countenance drew down his coat
            a          b             /a           b
```
(*Gawain* 335)

```
    C                 C        C        C
Parleys with the mariners, pays his money
    a                 b       /a        b
```
(*Patience* 99)

```
        C         C        C       C
And they set about briskly to bind on saddles
        a   (b)    b    /   b        a
```
(*Gawain* 1128)

I have put the *b* of *about*, above, in parenthesis because it is superfluous to the formal requirements of the line; in addition, it is brought in not by the poet's choice among descriptive alternatives but inadvertently, so to speak, by his use of an idiom requiring that adverb.

```
        C                 C          C   C
So send me over the rail into the rough sea
      (a) a                b  /       b   a
```
(*Patience* 211)

Rarely, all four chief syllables alliterate:

> C   C   C   C
> Sir Bors and Sir Bedivere, big men both
> a   a   /a   a
>
> (*Gawain* 554)

> C   C   C   C
> Now they tally their tokens; each takes one in turn
> a   a   /   a   a
>
> (*Patience* 193)

All the examples I have given so far can easily be read as having four chief syllables, and and these syllables alone participate in the alliterative pattern. But two related variant forms occur in which alliteration and chief stress do not coincide, and the frequency of their appearance in the alliterative verse of the *Gawain*-poet sets him apart from other poets. In one of these variants, at least one alliterating syllable, often the single one that is required in the second half-line, is an unstressed prefix:

> C   C   C   C
> "And that is best, I believe, and behooves me now"
> a   a   /   a   x
>
> (*Gawain* 1216)

> C   C   C   C
> As in the bottom of a boat where before he had slept
> a   a /   a   x
>
> (*Patience* 292)

In the other variant, the single alliterating syllable required in the second half-line is a word normally read with less stress than neighboring words in the sentence:

> C   C   C   C
> "The terms of this task too well you know"
> a   a /a   x
>
> (*Gawain* 546)

> C   C   C   C
> "Let the power of compassion put vengeance aside"
> a   a   /a   x
>
> (*Patience* 284)

Variants of this sort seem to appear more frequently in quoted speech than in the language of the narrator.

The Heavy Lines

A number of lines and groups of lines in *Gawain* and *Patience* exemplify a variant form of a different, and more important, sort. Its frequent and conspicuous presence, as with the variants just discussed, distinguishes the *Gawain*-poet from other poets of the alliterative tradition. In lines having this form, the count of stressed syllables exceeds in number the basic four. The first half-line, for example, may contain three such syllables. The metrical analysis of these heavy lines has been subject to debate, the main question being whether they should be read as having five stressed syllables of equal rank rather than four, and thus as divided into five measures, rather than four, in the musical sense. Consider, for example, the second line of each of the following passages:

> And since this Britain was built by this baron great,
> Bold boys bred there, in broils delighting,
> That did in their day many a deed most dire.
>
> > (*Gawain* 20–22)

> "I worship the one God whose will all obey:
> The wide world with the welkin, the wind and the stars,
> And all that range in that realm, he wrought with his word."
>
> > (*Patience* 206–8)

If equal rank were assigned to *bold*, *boys*, and *bred* in *Gawain* 21, and to *wide*, *world*, and *welkin* in *Patience* 207, the measure-bars preceding syllables perceived as occurring at temporally regular intervals would be placed thus:

> |Bold |boys |bred there, in |broils de|lighting

> The |wide |world with the |welkin, the |wind and the |stars

I contend, however, and have argued at length elsewhere,[2] that one of the three stressed syllables in these and other heavy first half-lines is subordinated to the other two; in linguistic terms, two syllables bear primary stress, and one secondary stress. I call syllables bearing primary stress "major chief," and those bearing secondary stress "minor chief," marking minor chief syllables with a lower-case *c*. I call unstressed syllables "intermediate" and leave them unmarked. The resultant patterns appear in metrical notation as follows (I have again added measure-bars to indicate the placement of the downbeats):

---

2. See "The Alliterative Long Line: The Extended Form" in *Sir Gawain and the Green Knight: A Stylistic and Metrical Study.*

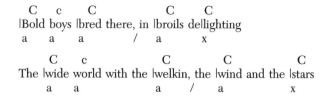

The first measures or units of these lines exemplify what I term compound meter, that is, the pattern includes two grades of stress, major and minor, as well as intermediate syllables such as "with the," rather than one, as in classical English verse. It should be noted that the second measure of *Patience* 206 is also compound, with major chief rank assigned to *one*, and minor to *God*.

An alternative reading of *Gawain* 21 might give *there* more emphasis than it receives in my scansion above, raising it, along with *boys*, to minor chief rank; the second measure as well as the first thus becomes compound. So too, *all* in *Patience* 206, might be scanned as a minor chief syllable. Such alternatives reflect differences of expressive emphasis rather than of metrical form; in both, the half-lines are divided into two measures, and compounding occurs.

The patterns I am describing are in fact familiar to us from nursery rhymes, jump-rope chants, and other popular forms of verse. The half-line "Bold boys bred there," read with minor chief as well as major chief syllables, is similar in pattern to the first half-line of "Baa baa black sheep, have you any wool?" Similarly, "the wide world and the welkin," if *wide* and *welkin* are read as major chief syllables and *world* as minor chief, has a pattern similar to that of "sing a song of sixpence." These popular verses exemplify compound meter; if we tap with a finger while reciting them at a normal pace, the taps will fall on the downbeats indicated below:

> C c C c C c C
> |"Baa baa |black sheep, |have you any |wool?"

> C c C c C c C
> |"Yes, sir, |yes, sir, |three bags |full."

This kinship is one aspect of the affinity between the long alliterative line and the language and poetry of everyday.[3]

---

3. The subordination of *boys* to *bold* and of *world* to *wide* accords also with a linguistic rule. In English, adjacent words of the four "open classes" (nouns, verbs, descriptive adjectives, and descriptive adverbs) do not both bear primary stress within a phrase; the stress given one of them is demoted to secondary. In sequences of adjective plus noun, for example, either the adjective or the noun will be subordinated, depending on whether the adjective has contrastive or emphatic as well as descriptive force. Thus, in the isolated clause "She lives in a white house," *house* receives primary stress and *white* secondary; in the sentence "She lives in a white house, but his house is gray," the order is reversed. In line 21 of *Gawain*, and line 207 of *Patience*, the adjectives *bold* and *wide* are rhetorically emphatic, as they might be in the spoken language in "He's a bold boy, that one" or "If you looked the wide world over you couldn't find its equal."

I am arguing that the triply stressed first half-lines that appear in the *Gawain*-poet's alliterative verse should be scanned as consisting not of three but of two measures, one or both of these being compound, with a demotion of one primary stress to secondary. But I am not arguing, be it noted, that the metrical patterns of *Sir Gawain* and *Patience* are compound throughout. There is a crucial difference between the alliterative verse of the *Gawain*-poet and the kind of verse we find in such nursery rhymes as "Baa, baa, black sheep"—a difference that in fact provides additional evidence for the scansion I am proposing. The difference is that compound measures in the *Gawain*-poet's lines are read in a context in which the basic form I described at the outset predominates, creating a rhythmical momentum, an ongoing "swing," of four simple measures per line to which the reader instinctively accommodates compound measures by accelerating them a little. If I were to rewrite *Gawain* 21 as "Bold boys bred there, that braved fierce foes," or *Patience* 207 as "The wide world and the welkin, the sun, moon, and stars," their meter would become compound in its entirety, like that of "Sing a song of sixpence, a pocket full of rye," and it has in fact been argued that the meter of these poems is of this sort. But a large majority of measures contain too few stressed syllables to permit us to read them as compound without distortion. In the second half-lines of *Gawain* 21 and *Patience* 207—"in broils delighting" and "the moon and the stars"—compound meter relaxes into simple combinations of stressed and unstressed syllables, in accordance with the prevailing norm. The same effect would be achieved by rewriting the nursery rhymes I have been quoting as "Sing a song of sixpence, pockets of rye," and "Baa baa black sheep, have you some wool?"

Variant Combinations of Alliteration and Stress in the Heavy Lines

In the two lines I have used as examples thus far, it is the first half-line in which compounding occurs, and all three stressed syllables alliterate. But compounding sometimes occurs in the second half-line; and the relation between alliteration, on the one hand, and major and minor (chief) rank, on the other hand, is variable. The examples that follow by no means illustrate all the possible permutations and combinations of the two aspects of the form.

Compounding in one or both halves of the line; alliteration on major chief syllables only:

```
        C       C    c    C   c  C
And Gawain the good knight in gay bed lies
        a       a    x    /   a  x   x
```
                                        (*Gawain* 1179)

```
      C         C          C     c   C
Or if the lord of my land, whose liege man I am
      a         a     /    a     x   x
```

Compounding, with alliteration lacking on minor or major chief syllables:

```
    C    c        C        C         C
Good couters and gay, and gloves of plate
    a    x        a   /    a         x
```

```
       C        C       C    c        C
"In His glory and grandeur—small gloom He feels"
       a        a     / x    a        x
```

(*Patience* 94)

```
    C    c        C          C         C
Sleet showered aslant upon shivering beasts
    x    a        x     /    a         x
```

(*Gawain* 2003)

In this last example, I have counted the alliteration of *sleet* with *aslant* as ornamental rather than as part of the formal pattern, because it does not link the two halves of the line.

```
   c       C     c    C          C          C
Yes, His gaze went wide enough, as he well might have known
   x       x    a    a    x   /    a              x
```

(*Patience* 117)

Rhymed Verse

Gawain is composed partly in alliterative and partly in rhymed verse. The poem is made up of 101 "paragraphs" of long alliterating lines. These are of varying length: the first five paragraphs contain 14, 12, 18, 20, and 17 long lines, respectively. Each group of long lines is finished off by a two-syllable line called the "bob," consisting of an unstressed syllable followed by a stressed one (in classical metrical terminology, an iamb), and a stanza called the "wheel," consisting of four lines of verse containing three measures or beats. The five lines rhyme *ababa*.

Pearl is composed entirely in rhymed verse. It is made up of 101 stanzas consisting of twelve lines, each containing four measures. The twelve lines rhyme *ababababbcbc*.

The metrical patterns of the rhyming lines of *Gawain* and *Pearl* can appropriately be called "mixed," since they have affinities both with native

alliterative verse and with the rhymed syllabic verse of Continental origin
first used in English by Chaucer. The lines are simple in form. In what can
be identified as a basic pattern having many variations, chief syllables alter-
nate with single intermediate syllables:

> x   C   x   C   x   C
> As lightning quick and light
>
> x   C   x C   x   C
> He looked to all at hand;
>
> x   C   x   C   x   C
> It seemed that no man might
>
>   x   C   x C   x   C
> His deadly dints withstand.

> (*Gawain* 199–202)

>   x   C   x   C x   C   x   C
> To that especial spot I hied
>
> x   C   x   C   x   C   x   C
> And entered that same garden green
>
> x   C   x   C x C x   C
> In August at a festive tide
>
>   x   C   x   C   x   C   x   C
> When corn is cut with scythe-edge keen.

> (*Pearl* 37–40)

As in the above examples, intermediate syllables are occasionally heavy (*man*
in *Gawain* 201, *-edge* in *Pearl* 40), but it is easy to identify three or four
chief syllables as the downbeats of three or four measures in each line. There
is thus no need, as there was in scanning the long alliterating lines, to invoke
the concept of "minor chief" rank as an alternative to inserting an additional
measure.

A feature of the mixed meter of the rhymed lines is the occasional pres-
ence of two intermediate syllables rather than one between chief syllables.
(In classical metrical terminology, the prevailing iambic meter is occasionally
varied by anapestic feet.) Entire wheels containing single intermediate syl-
lables only are rare in *Gawain*, as are sequences of four such lines in *Pearl*.

>   x   C   x x   C   x   C
> They linger and laugh awhile;
>
> x C   x   x   C   x   C
> She kisses the knight so true,
>
>   x   C   x   C   (x)x   C
> Takes leave in comeliest style

```
x   x  C     x  x     C   x C
```
And departs without more ado.

(*Gawain* 1554–57)

```
x  C   x  C     x    C x    C
```
My soul forsook that spot in space

```
x   C    x  C x x    C    x  C
```
And left my body on earth to bide.

```
x   C x   C   x   C    x     C
```
My spirit sped, by God's good grace,

```
x x    C    x    C  x    C x C
```
On a quest where marvels multiplied.

(*Pearl* 61–64)

An intermediate syllable and a chief syllable may change places at the beginning of the line. Such lines are said to begin with a "reversed foot."

```
C    x    x    C   x    C  x
```
Hold now your grim tool steady

(*Gawain* 413)

The above line has what is called a "feminine ending," that is, the rhyming word is disyllabic and adds a fourth intermediate syllable.

```
Cx    x  C   x   C    x C
```
"Duly the lord, at day's decline,

```
C   x   x  C x    C    x C
```
Said to the steward, 'Sir, proceed;' "

(*Pearl* 541–42)

The first intermediate syllable of a line may be omitted. Lines having this pattern are called "headless."

```
C   x   C    x    C
```
Bliss and hearth-fire bright

```
x  C    x  C x    C  x
```
Await the master's pleasure;

```
x    x   C  x    C   x  C
```
When the two men met that night,

```
C  x  C    x   C  x
```
Joy surpassed all measure.

(*Gawain* 1368–71)

```
C   x   C   x    C   x   C
```
"Less of bliss none brings us here

            x C   x C   x C x   C
Who bear the pearl upon our breast."

(Pearl 853–54)

As the above examples show, chief syllables regularly alternate with inter-
mediate syllables within the rhyming lines. In the rare cases where juxta-
position of chief syllables seems to occur, it can be avoided by the sounding
of a final -*e*, as frequently happens in Chaucerian verse. That the sounding
of -*e* is intentional is indicated by the fact that the first chief syllable of the
seemingly juxtaposed pair is invariably a word whose ancestral form had -*e*.
Such -*e*'s, like those that may have been sounded at the end of the long
alliterating line, represent an archaic mode of pronunciation handed down
in poetry from a time when syllabic -*e* was a feature of the spoken language.
The following examples are quoted from the original.

            x   C x C   x   C
Wyth rychë cote-armure

(Gawain 586)

            x   C x C   x C
He madë non abode

(Gawain 687)

            x   x   C   x C   x   C x   C x
The more strengthe of ioye myn hertë straynez

(Pearl 128)

In *Pearl* 128, the word *heart* (Old English *heorte*, Middle English *herte*)
ends in *e*. In my next example, it does not. This difference is due to the
inconsistent practice of the scribe, who copied out the poem at a time when
spelling had not yet become fixed. The poet surely intended in the latter
line, as in the earlier, to invoke an archaic pronunciation of the word with
two syllables to avoid the illegitimate pattern x C x C x C C. The line should
therefore be emended as follows:

            x   C   x   C   x C x   C
That dotz bot thrych my hert[ë] thrange
(literally, "That does but oppress my heart sorely")

(Pearl 17)

More often, words like *hert(e)* in the rhyming lines of *Gawain* and *Pearl* are
pronounced, in modern fashion, as monosyllables. This indicates that the
evolution of the language in the poet's northwest midland dialect had
reached a later stage than it had in Chaucer's London dialect: in Chaucer's
verse, such words are usually disyllabic. A radical difference between the
Gawain-poet and Chaucer in the treatment of -*e* in rhyme-words provides
further evidence to the same effect. Chaucer regularly rhymes words ending
in -*e* with other words ending in -*e*, the implication being that we are to

sound -e as a syllable in both members of a rhyming pair. The *Gawain*-poet rhymes words that have, or originally had, -e with words in whose ancestral forms -e is lacking, the implication being that -e is to remain silent in words of the former sort. Thus Chaucer rhymes *face*, *place*, and *space*, from French *facë*, *placë*, and *espacë*, respectively; the *Gawain*-poet also rhymes these words, but with them he combines *was* (Old English *wæs*) and *case* (Old French *cas*) in the sort of rhyme Chaucer does not use except when he is poking fun at "rym dogerel" in *Sir Thopas*.

In the mixed meter of the rhyming lines of *Gawain* and *Pearl*, formal metrical patterns correspond more closely to the natural stress-patterns of the spoken language than they do in the iambic meters of classical English poetry. That is, syllables having chief rank are also, as a rule, strongly stressed, while those of intermediate rank are weakly stressed. In iambic meter, such alternation is less regularly maintained. The following lines of Emily Dickinson's, for example, contain three iambic feet:

> The Brain, within its Groove,
> Runs evenly—and true—

The second chief syllable of each is lighter than the first and third; one is part of a preposition, the other an adverbial suffix. A reading that stressed them as heavily as the others would sound unnatural. Yet all three chief syllables in each line are formally equal, having one and the same metrical rank. Translated into the three-beat mixed meter of the wheels in *Gawain*, Dickinson's lines might run

> The brain, in its well-worn groove,
> Keeps to a constant course.

The strong, even rhythms generated by such sequences as this tend to impose themselves (though not, in a good reading, to the point of distortion) on sequences in which alternation between heavy and light syllables is less marked.

The four-beat lines of *Pearl* create a similar effect on a slightly larger scale. Here, a well-known passage from Robert Frost's "Stopping by Woods on a Snowy Evening" suggests itself for comparison:

> My little horse must think it queer
> To stop without a farmhouse near
> Between the woods and frozen lake
> The darkest evening of the year.

Translated into the mixed meter of *Pearl*, it might run thus:

> My horse in harnesss must think it queer
> To stop with never a farmhouse near
> 'Twixt wintry woods and ice-locked lake
> On the darkest night of all the year.

Here, as with the Dickinson lines, light chief syllables (the second syllables of *without* and *between, of*) have been replaced by heavier ones.

The rewritten passages differ from the originals in another, equally important way. In them, a number of pairs of chief syllables are linked by alliteration; repetition of sound adds to their conspicuousness as lexically weighty, and hence emphatic, parts of speech. Though alliteration is not a formal component of the verse in the rhyming lines of *Gawain* and *Pearl* as it is in the long lines, alliterative combinations frequently occur in them. In *Pearl*, however, alliteration is not equally distributed; certain passages have it in abundance, while in other passages it is scarce. (I present a passage of each type in the "Specimen Scansions," below.) We find something like the heavily alliterating four-beat lines of *Pearl* in modern poetry in Gerard Manley Hopkins's "Inversnaid:"

> This darksome burn, horseback brown,
> His rollrock highroad roaring down,
> In coop and in comb the fleece of his foam
> Flutes and low to the lake falls home.

But these lines are weightier still; a five-syllable sequence like "rollrock highroad roar-" is not found in *Pearl*.

Compared to the four-line subdivisions of the *Pearl* stanza, the four-line stanzas of the wheel in *Gawain* are notably terse: they offer succinct summary and comment after the continuity of the narrative or descriptive paragraphs of alliterating lines, which comes to a full stop with the bob. The three-beat line is the shortest line in which English poets have chosen to write entire poems, and the stanzas of the wheel are regularly divided into two halves, with a full stop at the end of the second line. In *Pearl*, the four-line subdivision is often a single syntactic unit (though there is usually a pause of at least comma strength at the end of each line, and a full stop at the end of every fourth line), and the three subdivisions of the stanza are themselves bound together by rhyme. Metrical units are marked off for the ear of the listener by repetition at regular intervals: the *b*-rhyme recurs at lines 2, 4, 6, 8, defining and linking the first two subdivisions, and a pivotal repetition of the *b*-rhyme in line 9 signals the beginning of the third, which rhymes *bcbc*. The second *c*-rhyme in each section is also the repeated, and thematically important, link-word; it is carried over from the fifth and last stanza to the first stanza of the next section, after which another takes its place.

The total effect, as the poem is heard or read in its entirety, is powerfully cumulative. The shift from link-word to link-word measures off in stages the rise in intensity of rhetoric and feeling, from the time of the introduction of the parable of the heavenly pearl in section XII until the dreamer rushes toward the stream at the beginning of section XX, rather like a series of shifts to the next higher musical key in successive choruses of a popular song.

Toward the end, we experience vicarously the resolution of the human drama, while recognizing, on the formal level, patterns of recurrence and return. Grasping the poem in the fullness of its mutually reinforcing meanings, we achieve a commensurate fullness of response.

Specimen Scansions

I have chosen two passages from *Gawain* and *Patience* and three from *Pearl*, presenting them first in the original, then in my translation. I quote the Middle English text of *Gawain* in the second edition, revised by Norman Davis, of the 1925 edition by J. R. R. Tolkien and E. V. Gordon (Clarendon Press, 1967), that of *Patience* as edited by J. J. Anderson (Manchester University Press, 1969) and that of *Pearl* as edited by E. V. Gordon (Clarendon Press, 1953). I have substituted *j* for *i*, *u* for *v*, and *v* for *u*, in accordance with modern spelling, and *th* for the Middle English letter *thorn*. For the Middle English letter *yogh*, I have substituted *y* at the beginnings of words and *gh* or *s/z* at the ends of words, depending on the sound represented.

From *Sir Gawain and the Green Knight*

Passage 1 and Passage 2 illustrate two different kinds of metrical effect. This difference in turn correlates with two differences that can be described statistically, in factual terms. The first passage, a description of Lord Bertilak's castle as Sir Gawain first sees it, contains, in the original poem, a sequence of five lines (785–89) in which a minor chief syllable is present in addition to the two major chief syllables of the first half-line. In my translation, there is a sequence of four such first half-lines (786–89). The second passage, taken from the conversation of the first bedroom scene, contains, in the original, no such half-lines. In my translation, there is one. In addition, the second passage contains, in the original, four sequences of three (or in one case, four) intermediate syllables between major chief syllables; there are five in my translation. The first passage contains only two such sequences (assuming that the -*ez* of *garytez* is not syllabic); there are two in my translation. The first passage is thus metrically heavier than the second; it contains a greater proportion of stressed to unstressed syllables and, as a result, is slower in pace.

"Clusters" of heavy lines appear in descriptive passages such as passage 1 and the description of the Green Knight when he first appears; sequences of lines that are comparatively light appear in passages of direct discourse, especially in conversations between Sir Gawain and the lady. The first effect seems to express the sustained impact of a remarkable sight on the beholder; the second, the fluency of casual repartee.

1. Lines 785–93

```
      C    c      C           C    C
The burne bode on bonk, that on blonk hoved,
      a    a      a    /      a    x

         C    c    C         C         C
Of the depe double dich that drof to the place;
         a    a    a    /    a         x

    C   c         C    C     C
The walle wod in the water wonderly depe,
    a   a         a   /a     x

    C        C    c      C         C
And eft a ful huge heght hit haled up on lofte,
    a        a    a    /  a        x

    C    c    C  C         C
Of harde hewen ston up to the tablez,
    a    a    x  /a        x

    C              C               C    C
Enbaned under the abataylment in the best lawe;
    a              a         /      a    x

         C          C    C      C
And sythen garytez ful gaye gered bitwene,
         a          a   /a      x

         C         C         C         C
Wyth mony luflych loupe that louked ful clene:
         a         a    /    a         x

    c    C           C    C          C
A better barbican that burne blusched upon never.
    a    a           a   /a           x
```

```
    C           C     C           C
The man on his mount remained on the bank
    a           a   / a           x

       C    c      C           C         C
Of the deep double moat that defended the place.
       a    a      x    /     a          x

    C   c         C    C      C
The wall went in the water wondrous deep,
    a   a         a   /a      x
```

          C   c   C   C   C
And a long way aloft it loomed overhead.
          a   x   a   /a   x

          C   c   C   C   C
It was built of stone blocks to the battlements' height,
          a   x   a   /   a   x

          C   C   C   C
With corbels under cornices in comeliest style;
          a   a   / a   x

     C   c   C   C   C
Watch-towers trusty protected the gate,
     x   a   a / a   x

          C   c   C   C   C
With many a lean loophole, to look from within:
          x   a   a   / a   x

     C   c   C   C   c   C
A better-made barbican the knight beheld never.
     a   x   a   /   b   a   b

2. Lines 1208-17

          C   C   C C
"God moroun, Sir Gawayn," sayde that gay lady,
     a   a   /   a   x

          C   C   C   C
"Ye ar a sleper unslyghe, that mon may slyde hider;
          a   a   /   a   x

          C   C   C   C
Now ar ye tan astyt! Bot true uus may schape,
          a   a / a   x

          C   C   C c   C
I schal bynde you in your bedde, that be ye trayst!"
          a   a   /x   a   x

     C   C   C   C
Al laghande the lady lanced tho bourdez.
     a   a /a   x

          C   C   C   C
"Goud moroun, gay," quoth Gawayn the blythe,
     a   a   /   a   x

    C   C   C   c C
"Me schal worthe at your wille, and that me wel lykez,
      a   a   /   x   a   x

  C   C   C   C
For I yelde me yederly, and yeghe after grace,
   a   a   /   a   x

      C   C   C   C
And that is the best, be my dome, for my byhovez nede!"
         a   a   x   /   a   x

       C   C   C   c   C
And thus he bourded ayayn with mony a blythe laghter.
         a   x /   x   a   x

    C   C   C C
"Good morning, Sir Gawain," said that gay lady,
a   a   /   a   x

   C   c   C   C   C
"A slack sleeper you are, to let one slip in!
 a   a   x / x   a   x

      C   C   C   C
Now you are taken in a trice—a truce we must make,
        a   a / a   x

     C   C   C   C
Or I shall bind you in your bed, of that be assured."
      a   a / x   a   x

   C   C   C C
Thus laughing lightly that lady jested.
   a   a   /   a   x

    C   C   C   C
"Good morning, good lady," said Gawain the blithe,
a   a   /   a   x

   C   C   C   C
"Be it with me as you will; I am well content!
 a   a /   a   x

    C   C   C   C
For I surrender myself, and sue for your grace,
   a   a /   a   x

```
        C         C            C            C
And that is best, I believe, and behooves me now."
        a         a      /     a           x
```

```
    C        C            C        C
Thus jested in answer that gentle knight.
    a        x      /     a        x
```

From *Patience*

1. Lines 137–44

```
    C   c          C   c        C      C
An-on out of the north-east the noys bigynes,
    a    b         a    b  /    a      x
```

```
        C      c            C            C  C
When bothe brethes con blowe upon blo watteres;
        a      a            a      /     a  x
```

```
    C   c          C        C           C
Rogh rakkes ther ros with rudnyng an-under,
a    a            a  /     a           x
```

```
        C   c         C        C        C
The see soghed ful sore, gret selly to here.
        a   a         a  /      a        x
```

```
        C                 C      c        C            C
The wyndes on the wonne water so wrastel to-geder
        a                 a      a  /     a            x
```

```
            C          C   C           C
That the wawes ful wode waltered so highe
            a          a   /a          x
```

```
            C                 C            C  C
And efte busched to the abymne, that breed fysches
            a                 a      /     a  x
```

```
        C            C   C           C
Durst nowhere for rogh arest at the bothem.
        x            a   / a          x
```

```
    C   c          C   c        C      C
And now out of the northeast the noise begins
    a    b         a    b  /    a      x
```

    C   c   C   C   C
As they blow with both their breaths over bleak waters;
     a   a   a   /   a   x

    C   c   c   C   C   C
The cloud-rack runs ragged, reddening beneath;
 x   a   a   a   /a   x

    C   c   C   C   C
The ocean howls hellishly, awful to hear;
 a   a   a   /a   a

    C   C   c   C   C
The winds on the wan water so wildly contend
 a   a   a   /   a   x

     C   C   C   C
That the surges ascending are swept up so high
     a   a   /   a   x

        C   c   C   C   c   C
And then drawn back to the depths, that fear-dazed fish
       a   x   a   /   x   a   x

    C   C   C   c   C
Dare not rest, for that rage, at the roiled sea-bottom.
   a   a   /   a   x   x

2. Lines 413–24

  C   C   C C
I biseche the, syre, now thou self jugge,
 a   a   /   a   x

    C   c   C   C   C
Watz not this ilk my worde that worthen is nouthe,
a   b   x   a   /   a   b

    C   C   C   c   C
That I kest in my cuntre, when thou thy carp sendez,
    a   a   /   x   a   x

        C   C   C   C
That I schulde tee to thys toun thi talent to preche?
       a   a   /   a   x

   C   C   C C
Wel knew I thi cortaysye, thy quoynt suffraunce,
 a   a   /   a   x

    C   C   C   C
Thy bounte of debonerte and thy bene grace,
    a   a   /   a   x

    C   c   C   C   C
Thy longe abydyng wyth lur, thy late vengaunce,
    a   x   a / a   x

        C   C   C   C
And ay thy mercy is mete, be mysse never so huge.
        a   a / a   x

  c   C   C   C   C
I wyst wel, when I hade worded quat-so-ever I cowthe
a   a   (a)   a   /a   x   x

    C   c   C   c   C   c   C
To manace alle thise mody men that in this mote dowellez,
    a   b   a   a / b   a   x

      C   C   C C
Wyth a prayer and a pyne thayt myght her pese gete,
      a   a   /   a   x

    C   C   C   C
And ther-fore I wolde haf flowen fer in-to Tarce.
    a   a   /a   x

NOTE: In line 418, *debonerte* is stressed on the second syllable, and the final
e is syllabic, as also in *bounte*.

    C   C   C   C
I beseech you now, Sire, yourself be the judge:
    a   a / a   x

  C   C   C   C
Were they not my words that forewarned of this change,
a   a /   a   x

     C   C   C   C
That I said when you summoned me to sail from Judea
     a   a   / a   x

    C   C   C   C
To travel to this town and teach them your will?
(a) a   (a)   a /   a   x

    C   c   C   c   C   C
I knew well your courteous ways, your wise forbearance,
    x   a   x   a /   a   x

```
      C           C           C           C
Your abounding beneficence, the bounty of your grace,
      a         a x         /     a             x

      C           C                 C     C
Your leniency, your longsuffering, your delayed vengeance;
      a           a              /    a     x

            C           C               C   c     C
And ever mercy in full measure, though the misdeed be huge.
            a           a       /          a   x     x

      C                 C           C           C
I knew well, when I had wielded such words as I could
      a                 a       /   a           x

   C               C     c     C               C
To menace all these mighty men, the masters of this place,
   a               a     a  /   a               x

            C           C                   C           C
That for a prayer and a penance you would pardon them all,
            a           a       /           a           x

      C                     C   c C       C
And therefore I would have fled far off into Tarshish.
      x    (a)                a  /a x       x
```

From *Pearl*

To illustrate the metrical patterns of *Pearl*, I have chosen the opening stanza, a stanza from the pearl-maiden's argument immediately following her narration of the parable of the vineyard, and a stanza from the dreamer's vision of the celestial Jerusalem.

The "rules" determining scansions are as described above. The inflectional endings *-ed* (as in *jugged* "judged") and *-ez* (as in *sydez* "sides") had continued to be pronounced as syllables in the language of the *Pearl*-poet and are often used by him to provide the necessary intermediate syllables within the line. They could also be contracted, as indicated by their presence in lines where their sounding would result in irregular sequences of three intermediate syllables. Where they are followed by a single intermediate syllable, I have left their metrical status indeterminate, though I am inclined to think that they should be contracted in most, if not all, such cases. I have left *-ez* silent in *hondelyngez* in example 2, on the linguistic grounds that in this word it falls after a syllable bearing less than primary stress; cf. the pronunciation indicated by the meter for *planetez* in example 3.

1. Lines 1–12

c x   c x   x   c   x   c
Perle, plesaunte to prynces paye,

x   c   x   c   x   c   x   c
To clanly clos in golde so clere,

c   x c(x)x   x   c   x x c
Oute of oryent, I hardyly saye,

x   c(x) x   c x   x   c x   c
Ne proved I never her precios pere.

x c   x c x   x c   x c
So rounde, so reken in uche araye,

x   c   x   c   x   c x   c
So smal, so smothe her sydez were,

x   x c x   x c   x   c   x   c
Quere-so-ever I jugged gemmez gaye,

x c   x   c   x   c   x   c
I sette hyr sengeley in synglere.

x c   x c   x c x x c
Allas! I leste hyr in on erbere;

x   c   x   c   x   c x c
Thurgh gresse to grounde hit fro me yot.

x   c   x   c (x)   x   c   x   c
I dewyne, fordolked of luf-daungere

x   x   c x c   x c x   c
Of that pryvy perle wythouten spot.

NOTE: In line 1, *perle* was probably pronounced very much like modern English *peril*.

c   x x   c   x   c   x c
Pearl, that a prince is well content

x c   x c x x   c   x   c
To give a circle of gold to wear,

c   x x c   x   c x c
Boldly I say, all orient

x   c   x   c x   c   x c
Brought forth none precious like to her;

```
x  c    xx  c    x c  x  c
```
So comely in every ornament,

```
x  c  x  x  c     x   c     x    c
```
So slender her sides, so smooth they were,

```
c x   x  c    x  c    x    c
```
Ever my mind was bound and bent

```
x c  x  x c    x c  x  c
```
To set her apart without a peer.

```
x  x  c  x  x  c   x c   x  c
```
In a garden of herbs I lost my dear;

```
x      c  x  c    x c x    c
```
Through grass to ground away it shot;

```
x   c   x    x c x c  x c
```
Now, lovesick, the heavy loss I bear

```
x   x c x  c    x c  x   c
```
Of that secret pearl without a spot.

2. Lines 673–84

```
x     c x  c    x c  x  c
```
"Ryght thus I knaw wel in this cas,

```
c  x  x c   x  c   x  c
```
Two men to save is god by skylle:

```
x c    x    c    x  c  x  c
```
The ryghtwys man schal se hys face,

```
x  c   x   c x    x  c   x    c
```
The harmlez hathel schal com hym tylle.

```
x  c x  x  c    c   x x  c
```
The Sauter hyt satz thus in a pace:

```
c      x   x   c     x  c  x  c
```
'Lorde, quo schal klymbe thy hygh[e] hylle,

```
x  (x)  c   x  c     x  c x  c
```
Other rest wythinne thy holy place?'

```
x   c   x   c   x c  x  c
```
Hymself toonsware he is not dylle:

```
c   x    c     x  c  x c
```
'Hondelyngez harme that dyt not ille,

```
        x  c  x   c   x    c   x    c
```
That is of hert bothe clene and lyght,

```
        c   x  x   c x   c  x  c
```
Ther schal hys step[e] stable stylle':

```
        x c   x x   c x  c   x c
```
The innosent is ay saf by ryght.

NOTE: *Hygh* (6) and *step* (11) have been emended to provide a necessary intermediate syllable; cf. the general discussion of the metrical form, above. Note the rhyme *cas: face*, evidence that *-e* in *face* is silent as in modern English.

```
         x   c   x    c x c   x  c
```
"I know right reason in this case

```
         x    c  x  c  x   c x c
```
And thereto cite authority:

```
          x  c  x    c   x   c  x  c
```
The righteous man shall see his face

```
          x    x c  x x    c   x    c   x c
```
And the innocent bear him company.

```
          c x  x  c    x   c x  c
```
So in a verse the psalter says,

```
          c     x  x   c    x   c x   c
```
'Lord, who shall climb your hill on high

```
          x   c    x  c   x    c x c
```
Or rest within your holy place?'

```
          x    c  x x   c   x  c    x c
```
And readily then he makes reply:

```
          c     x   c   x c  x c
```
'Hands that did no injury,

```
          c     x   x  c  x    c   x   c
```
Heart that was always pure and light:

```
          c    x   x   c   x  c   x  c
```
There shall his steps be stayed in joy';

```
          x c   x c  x   c    x  c
```
The innocent is safe by right.

3. *Lines 1069–80*

```
    x   c   x   x c x c    x   c
```
The mone may therof acroche no myghte;

```
    x   c   x c  x   c x x   c
```
To spotty ho is, of body to grym,

```
x   c x   c x   c x   c
```
And also ther is never nyght.

```
        c   x    x   c    x   c   x   c
```
What schulde the mone ther compas clym?

```
x    x c x   c    x   c   x c
```
And to even wyth that worthly lyght

```
    x    c (x) x c    x   c x    c
```
That schynez upon the brokez brym

```
    x   c x   x   c   x c    x   c
```
The planetez arn in to pouer a plyght

```
x    x c x   c    x c x c
```
And the sel[ve] sunne ful fer to dym.

```
x c    x   c x x    c x    c
```
Aboute that water arn tres ful schym,

```
    x   c    x   x c x   c   x   c
```
That twelve frytez of lyf con bere ful sone;

```
    c   x    x   c   x   c(x)  x   c
```
Twelve sythez on yer thay beren ful frym,

```
x    x c x   c x c    x   c
```
And renowlez nwe in uche a mone.
```

NOTE: *Self* (8) has been emended to *selve*, a disyllablic "weak" form following the definite article. Cf. Chaucer's line "Right in that selvë wisë, soth to seyë" (*Troilus* 3.355).

```
    x   c   x c   x   c   x c
```
The moon has in that reign no right;

```
    x   c x   x c   x   c x x   c
```
Too spotty she is, of body austere;

```
    x   c   x   c   x   c   x c
```
And they who dwell there know no night—

```
    x   c x c   x   c x   c
```
Of what avail her varying sphere?
```

```
x    c   x c   x   c   x   c
```
And set beside that wondrous light

```
 x    c    x c   x   c x    c
```
That shines upon the waters clear

```
 x   c x   x    c    x   c   x   c
```
The planets would lose their lustre quite

```
x      x  c  x c   x      c    x   c
```
And the sun itself would pale appear.

```
 x c     x c x  x     c     x    c
```
Beside the river are trees that bear

```
 c     x    x c    x    c     x c
```
Twelve fruits of life their boughs upon;

```
 c    x    x  c    x   c x      c
```
Twelve times a year they burgeon there

```
x     x c   x   c     x   c   x   c
```
And renew themselves with every moon.

Suggestions for Further Reading

Bennett, M. J. *Community, Class, and Careerism: Cheshire and Lancashire Society in the Age of Sir Gawain and the Green Knight.* Cambridge, 1983.

Benson, L. D. *Art and Tradition in Sir Gawain and the Green Knight.* Brunswick, NJ: Rutgers University Press, 1965.

Blanch, Robert J., ed. *Sir Gawain and Pearl: Critical Essays.* Bloomington: Indiana University Press, 1966.

Borroff, Marie. *Sir Gawain and the Green Knight: A Stylistic and Metrical Study.* New Haven, Conn.: Yale University Press, 1962.

Brewer, Derek, and Jonathan Gibson, eds. *A Companion to the Gawain-Poet.* Cambridge, UK: D. S. Brewer, 1997.

Burrow, J. A. *A Reading of Sir Gawain and the Green Knight.* London: Routledge, 1965.

Fox, Denton. *Twentieth Century Interpretations of Sir Gawain and the Green Knight: A Collection of Critical Essays.* Englewood Cliffs, NJ: Prentice-Hall, 1968.

Lawton, David E., ed. *Middle English Alliterative Poetry and Its Literary Background: Seven Essays.* Cambridge, UK: D. S. Brewer, 1982.

Patience. Ed. J. J. Anderson. Manchester, UK: Manchester University Press, 1969. Scholarly edition of the original poem.

Pearl. Ed. E. V. Gordon. Oxford, UK: Clarendon Press, 1953. Scholarly edition of the original poem.

The Poems of the Pearl Manuscript: Pearl, Cleanness, Patience, Sir Gawain and the Green Knight. Ed. Malcolm Andrew and Ronald Waldron. Exeter, UK: Exeter University Press, 1987. Scholarly edition of the four poems.

Sir Gawain and the Green Knight. Ed. J. R. R. Tolkien and E. V. Gordon. Rev. ed. Norman Davis. Oxford, UK: Clarendon Press, 1967. Scholarly edition of the original poem.

Spearing, A. C. *The Gawain-Poet: A Critical Study.* Cambridge, UK: Cambridge University Press, 1970.